THE TRANSFORMATION OF INTIMACY

THE TRANSFORMATION OF INTIMACY

Sexuality, Love and Eroticism in Modern Societies

Anthony Giddens

Stanford University Press
Stanford, California

Stanford University Press
Stanford, California
© 1992 Anthony Giddens
Originating publisher: Polity Press, Cambridge,
  in association with Blackwell Publishers, Oxford
First published in the U.S.A. by
  Stanford University Press, 1992
Printed in the United States of America
Cloth ISBN 0-8047-2090-8
Paper ISBN 0-8047-2214-5

This book is printed on acid-free paper.

Original printing 1992
Last figure below indicates year of this printing:
08   07   06   05   04   03   02   01   00

CONTENTS

———

PREFACE

———

A number of people have read, and commented upon, earlier drafts of this book. I have tried to take account of most of the criticisms they raised in so far as it was within my capacity to do so. I would like especially to thank the following: Grant Barnes, Michèle Barrett, Teresa Brennan, Montserrat Guiberneau, Rebecca Harkin, David Held, Sam Hollick, Graham McCann, Heather Warwick, Jeffrey Weeks and an anonymous reviewer of Stanford University Press. I would also like to thank Avril Symonds for her work on the preparation of the manuscript and Helen Jeffrey for her very conscientious copy-editing.

I wanted to produce a book which would be accessible to most readers who might care to pick it up. So I have avoided technical verbiage whenever possible, even when I stray into intellectual areas of some complexity. I have made use of a wide variety of sources, but in the interests of readability I have kept references and footnotes to a minimum. One resource upon which I have drawn extensively perhaps needs some comment here: the literature of self-help. Scorned by many, to me it offers insights unavailable elsewhere and I deliberately stay as close to the *genre* as possible in developing my own arguments.

INTRODUCTION

———

Sexuality: a subject which might seem a public irrelevance – an absorbing, but essentially private, concern. A constant factor also, one might imagine, since it is given by biology and necessary for the continued life of the species. Yet in fact sex now continually features in the public domain and, moreover, speaks the language of revolution. Over the past several decades, so it is said, a sexual revolution has occurred; and revolutionary hopes have been pinned to sexuality by many thinkers, for whom it represents a potential realm of freedom, unsullied by the limits of present-day civilisation.

How should one interpret such claims? That question prompted me to write this book. I set out to write on sex. I found myself writing just as much about love; and about gender. Works on sex themselves tend to be gendered. In some of the most notable studies of sexuality written by men there is virtually no mention of love, and gender appears as something of an addendum. Today, for the first time in history, women claim equality with men. In what follows I don't attempt to analyse how far gender inequalities persist in the economic or political domains. I concentrate instead upon an emotional order where women – ordinary women, going about their day-to-day lives, as well as self-consciously feminist groups – have pioneered changes of great, and generalisable, importance. These concern essentially an exploration of the potentialities of the 'pure relationship', a relationship of sexual and emotional equality, which is explosive in its connotations for pre-existing forms of gender power.

The rise of romantic love provides a case-study of the origins of the pure relationship. Ideals of romantic love have long affected the aspirations of women more than those of men, although of course men have not been uninfluenced by them. The ethos of romantic love has had a double impact upon women's situation. On the one hand it has helped to put women 'in their place' – the home. On the other hand, however, romantic love can be seen as an active, and radical, engagement with the 'maleness' of modern society. Romantic love presumes that a durable emotional tie can be established with the other on the basis of qualities intrinsic to that tie itself. It is the harbinger of the pure relationship, although it also stands in tension with it.

The emergence of what I term plastic sexuality is crucial to the emancipation implicit in the pure relationship, as well as to women's claim to sexual pleasure. Plastic sexuality is decentred sexuality, freed from the needs of reproduction. It has its origins in the tendency, initiated somewhere in the late eighteenth century, strictly to limit family size; but it becomes further developed later as the result of the spread of modern contraception and new reproductive technologies. Plastic sexuality can be moulded as a trait of personality and thus is intrinsically bound up with the self. At the same time – in principle – it frees sexuality from the rule of the phallus, from the overweening importance of male sexual experience.

Modern societies have a covert emotional history, yet to be fully drawn into the open. It is a history of the sexual pursuits of men, kept separate from their public selves. The sexual control of women by men is much more than an incidental feature of modern social life. As that control starts to break down, we see the compulsive character of male sexuality more plainly revealed – and this declining control also generates a rising tide of male violence towards women. At the moment, an emotional abyss has opened up between the sexes, and one cannot say with any certainty how far it will be bridged.

Yet the radicalising possibilities of the transformation of intimacy are very real. Some have claimed that intimacy can be oppressive, and clearly this may be so if it is regarded as a demand for constant emotional closeness. Seen, however, as a transactional negotiation of personal ties by equals, it appears in a completely different light. Intimacy implies a wholesale democratising of the interpersonal domain, in a manner fully compatible with democracy in the public sphere. There are further implications as well. The transformation of intimacy might be a subversive influence upon modern institutions as a whole. For a social world in which emotional fulfilment replaced the maximising of economic growth would be very different from that which we know at present. The changes now affecting sexuality are indeed revolutionary, and in a very profound way.

1

EVERYDAY EXPERIMENTS, RELATIONSHIPS, SEXUALITY

In his novel *Before She Met Me*, Julian Barnes discusses the fate of one Graham Hendrick, an academic historian, who has left his wife and begun a relationship with another woman. When the novel opens, Graham is in his late thirties, has been married fifteen years and, 'halfway through life', he can 'feel the downhill slope already'. At an otherwise run-of-the-mill party he meets Ann, who once was a small-time film actress and has since become a fashion buyer. For some reason their encounter stirs in him barely remembered feelings of hope and excitement. He feels 'as if some long-broken line of communication to a self of twenty years ago had suddenly been restored' and is 'once more capable of folly and idealism'.

After a series of clandestine meetings, which turn into a full-blown affair, Graham leaves his wife and child and sets up house with Ann. Once his divorce comes through the two marry. The core of the novel concerns Graham's progressive discovery of the lovers in Ann's life before he entered it. She hides little, but volunteers no information unless he asks for it directly. Graham gradually becomes obsessed with a need to uncover the sexual details of Ann's past. He watches and rewatches the cameo parts Ann has played on the screen, trying to glimpse an exchange of glances, or other signs, that would indicate that she and a particular man with whom she appeared had been lovers. Sometimes she admits there have been sexual liaisons, mostly she insists not.

The ultimate development of the story is savage, its conclusion almost completely subverting the style of dead-pan humour in which most of the book is written. By dint of assiduous research, Graham discovers that his best friend, Jack – to whom he had been confiding his problems about Ann's life 'before she met me' – himself had a sexual involvement with Ann several years before. Graham arranges to see his friend as if to continue his discussions. But he takes with him a knife, a 'six-inch blade tapering from a breadth of an inch to a sharp point'. When Jack turns his back on him at one point, to busy himself with a minor task, Graham stabs him. As Jack turns round in bewilderment, Graham slips the knife in repeatedly, 'between the heart and the genitals'. After putting a plaster on his finger where he has cut it during the course of the murder, he settles down in a chair with the remnants of a cup of coffee that Jack had made for him.

In the meantime, increasingly worried by Graham's absence, which has stretched across the night, and having telephoned the police and local hospitals in a fruitless endeavour to discover his whereabouts, Ann starts searching through Graham's desk. There she unearths documents bearing witness to Graham's compulsive enquiries into her past – and finds that he knows of her affair with Jack (the one sexual encounter which she has actively concealed from Graham). She goes over to Jack's flat and finds Graham there, together with Jack's bloodstained body. Without understanding why, she lets Graham calm her down and tie her arms together with a few yards of washing-line. Graham calculates that this procedure will give him enough time to accomplish his objective, before she can dash to the phone to get help. 'No curtain lines; no melodrama': picking up the knife, Graham cuts deeply into each side of his throat.

About Ann – 'he loved Ann, there wasn't any doubt about that' – he has miscalculated. Ann dives headfirst through the glass of a window, screaming loudly. By the time the police arrive, the armchair is irretrievably soaked with blood and Graham is dead. The implication of the concluding paragraphs of the novel is that Ann has killed herself also – inadvertently or otherwise we do not know.

Before She Met Me is not primarily a novel about jealousy. While reading through the materials that Graham has accumulated about her, Ann recognises that jealous 'was a word she wouldn't use of him'. The important thing was that 'he couldn't handle her past'.[1] The ending is violent – incongruously so given the half-comic tone of the rest of the book – but cool. Graham's violence is a frustrated attempt at mastery. Its origins are left quite opaque by the novelist, something which reflects their obscurity to Graham himself. The secrets Graham seeks to discover in Ann's sexual history are bound up with her non-conformity to what he expects of a woman – her past is incompatible with his ideals. The problem is an emotional one; he recognises how absurd it is to suppose that Ann should have organised her former life in anticipation of meeting him. Yet her sexual independence, even when he did not 'exist' for her, is unacceptable, to such a degree that the end-result is a violent destructiveness. To his credit, Graham tries to shield Ann from the violence she has provoked in him; but of course she becomes caught up in it anyhow.

The events described in the novel are distinctly contemporary; as a discussion of the lives of ordinary people, the novel could not have been set, say, a century ago. For it presumes a significant degree of sexual equality and, specifically, depends upon the fact that today it is commonplace for a woman to have multiple lovers prior to entering (and even during, as well as after leaving) a 'serious' sexual involvement. Of course, there have always been a minority of women for whom sexual variety, and also a measure of equality, were possible. But for the most part women have been divided into the virtuous and the loose, and 'loose women' have existed only on the margins of respectable society. 'Virtue' has long been defined in terms of a woman's refusal to succumb to sexual temptation, a refusal bolstered by various institutional protections, such as chaperoned courting, shotgun marriages and so forth.

Men, on the other hand, have traditionally been regarded – and not only by themselves – as requiring sexual variety for their physical health. It has generally been thought acceptable for men to engage in multiple sexual encounters before marriage, and the double standard after marriage was a very real phenomenon. As Lawrence Stone says in his study of the history of divorce in England, until quite recently a rigid dual standard existed about the sexual experience of men and women. A single act of adultery by a wife was 'an unpardonable breach of the law of property and the idea of hereditary descent' and discovery brought into play highly punitive measures. Adultery on the part of husbands, by contrast, was widely 'regarded as a regrettable but understandable foible'.[2]

In a world of increasing sexual equality – even if such equality is far from complete – both sexes are called upon to make fundamental changes in their outlooks on, and behaviour towards, one another. The adjustments demanded of women are considerable but, perhaps because the novelist is male, these are neither fully represented, nor portrayed with much sympathy, in the book. Barbara, Graham's first wife, is depicted as a shrill, demanding creature, whose attitudes he finds baffling; while he feels a consistent love for Ann, his understanding of her views and actions is hardly any deeper. One could even say that, in spite of the intensive research work which he carries out on Ann's prior life, he does not really come to know her at all.

Graham tends to dismiss the behaviour of Barbara and Ann in a traditional way: women are emotional, whimsical beings, whose thought-processes do not move along rational lines. Yet he has compassion for both of them, particularly, at the time of the story, Ann. His new wife is not a 'loose woman', nor has he any right to treat her as such. When she goes to see Jack, after having married Graham, she firmly rejects the advances Jack makes to her. Yet Graham cannot shake from his mind the threat he feels from activities which occurred before he was 'in control' of her.

The novelist conveys very well the tentative, open-ended nature of Graham's second marriage, which differs substantially from his first. Graham's earlier marriage, it is made clear, was more of a 'naturally given' phenomenon, based on the conventional division between housewife and male breadwinner. With Barbara, marriage was a state of affairs, a not particularly rewarding part of life, like having a job that one does not especially appreciate, but dutifully carries on. Marriage to Ann, by contrast, is a complex series of interactions that have to be constantly negotiated and 'worked through'.[3] In his second marriage, Graham has entered a new world that was only barely emerging at the time of his youth. It is a world of sexual negotiation, of 'relationships', in which new terminologies of 'commitment' and 'intimacy' have come to the fore.

Before She Met Me is a novel about male disquiet, and male violence, in a social world undergoing profound transformations. Women no longer go along with male sexual dominance, and both sexes must deal with the implications of this phenomenon. Personal life has become an open project, creating new demands and anxieties. Our interpersonal existence is being thoroughly transfigured, involving us all in what I shall call *everyday social experiments*, with which wider social changes more or less oblige us to engage. Let us give some more sociological flesh to these changes, which are to do with marriage and the family as well as with sexuality directly.

Social change and sexual behaviour

Lillian Rubin studied the sexual histories of almost a thousand heterosexual people in the US aged between eighteen and forty-eight in 1989. In so doing, she produced evidence revealing 'a tale of change of almost staggering proportions in relations between men and women' over the past few decades.[4] The early sexual lives of respondents over forty contrasted dramatically with those reported by younger age-groups. The author prefaces her report on what things were like for the older generation with her own testimony, as a member of that generation herself. She was a virgin at the time of her marriage during World War II, a girl who 'followed all the rules of her day', and would never have 'gone all the way'. She wasn't alone in drawing clear boundaries to mark out the limits of sexual exploration, but shared codes of conduct common to her friends. Her prospective husband was an active participant in ensuring that those codes were complied with; his sense of sexual 'rights and wrongs' matched her own.

Virginity on the part of girls prior to marriage was prized by both sexes. Few girls disclosed the fact if they allowed a boyfriend to have full sexual intercourse – and many were only likely to permit such an act to happen once formally engaged to the boy in question. More sexually active girls were disparaged by the others, as well as by the very males who sought to 'take advantage' of them. Just as the social reputation of the girls rested upon their ability to resist, or contain, sexual advances, that of the boys depended upon the sexual conquests they could achieve. Most boys gained such conquests only by, as one 45-year-old respondent put it, 'fooling around with one of *those* girls, the sluts'.

When we look at teenage sexual activity today, the good girl/bad girl distinction still applies to some degree, as does the ethic of male conquest. But other attitudes, on the part of many teenage girls in particular, have changed quite radically. Girls feel they have an entitlement to engage in sexual activity, including sexual intercourse, at whatever age seems appropriate to them. In Rubin's survey, virtually no teenage girls talk of 'saving themselves' for an anticipated engagement and marriage. Instead, they speak a language of romance and commitment which acknowledges the potentially finite nature of their early sexual involvements. Thus, in response to a question from Rubin about her sexual activities with her boyfriend, one sixteen-year-old interviewee remarked, 'We love each other, so there's no reason why we shouldn't be making love.' Rubin then asked to what extent she envisaged a long-term tie with her partner. Her reply was: 'Do you mean are we going to get married? The answer is no. Or will we be together next year? I don't know about that; that's a long time from now. Most kids don't stay together for such a long time. But we won't date anybody else as long as we're together. That's a commitment, isn't it?'[5]

In previous generations, the conventional practice was for the sexually active teenage girl to play the part of innocent. This relation is today usually reversed: innocence, where necessary, plays the role of sophisticate. According to Rubin's findings, changes in the sexual behaviour and attitudes of girls have been much more pronounced than among boys. She did talk to some boys who were sensitive about connections between sex and commitment, and who resisted the equation of sexual success and male prowess. Most, however, spoke admiringly of male friends who went with lots of girls, while condemning girls who did the same. A few girls in Rubin's sample emulated traditional male sexual behaviour, did so openly and with some defiance; faced with such actions, the majority of boys responded with a sense of outrage. They still wanted innocence, at least of a sort. Several young women whom Rubin interviewed, on the point of getting married, found it necessary to lie to their future spouses about the range of their earlier sexual experiences.

One of the most striking findings of Rubin's research, which is echoed by other surveys and applies across all age-groups, is the expanded variety of sexual activities in which most people either engage or deem it appropriate for others to participate in if they so wish. Thus among the women and men over forty, fewer than one in ten had engaged in oral sex during adolescence; for each successive generation, the proportion increases. Among the current generation of teenagers, although not universally practised, oral sex is regarded as a normal part of sexual behaviour. Every adult Rubin interviewed now had at least some experience with it – this in a society where oral sex is still described as 'sodomy' in statute books and is actually illegal in twenty-four states.

Men mostly welcome the fact that women have become more sexually available, and claim that in any longer-term sexual tie they want a partner who is intellectually and economically their equal. Yet, according to Rubin's findings, they show obvious and deep-seated unease when faced with the implications of such preferences. They say that women have 'lost the capacity for kindness', that they 'don't know how to compromise any more' and that 'women today don't want to be wives, they want wives'. Men declare they want equality, but many also make statements suggesting that they either reject, or are nervous about, what it means for them. 'How would you contribute to raising the children?' Rubin asked Jason, a man who, in his own words, has 'no problem with strong aggressive women'. His answer: 'I'm certainly willing to do all I can. I don't expect to be an absent father, but someone has to take the larger share of responsibility . . . And I won't say I can do that, because I can't. I have my career, and it's very important to me, what I've worked for all my life.'[6]

Most people, women and men, now come to marriage bringing with them a substantial fund of sexual experience and knowledge. Not for them the abrupt transition between furtive fumblings or illicit encounters and the more secure, yet also often more demanding, sexuality of the marriage bed. Newly wed marriage partners today are for the most part sexually experienced, and there is no period of sexual apprenticeship in the early stages of the marriage, even when the individuals involved have not lived with one another previously.

Yet far more is anticipated sexually of marriage, Rubin shows, by both women and men, than was normally the case in earlier generations. Women expect to receive, as well as provide, sexual pleasure, and many have come to see a rewarding sex life as a key requirement for a satisfactory marriage. The proportion of women married for more than five years who have had extramarital sexual encounters is today virtually the same as that of men. The double standard still exists, but women are no longer tolerant of the view that, while men need variety and can be expected to engage in extramarital adventures, they should not behave likewise.

How much can we glean about generic social changes from such a piece of research, carried out with limited numbers of people, in a single country? We can learn, I think, essentially what we need to know for the purposes of this study. It is beyond dispute that, broadly speaking, developments of the sort charted by Rubin are happening throughout most Western societies – and to some extent in other parts of the world as well. Of course, there are significant divergencies between different countries, sub-cultures and socio-economic strata. Certain groups, for example, stand apart from the sort of changes described, or actively attempt to resist them. Some societies have a longer history of sexual tolerance than others and the changes which they are experiencing are perhaps not quite as radical as in the US. In many, however, such transitions are happening against the backdrop of more constraining sexual values than were characteristic of American society several decades ago. For people living in these contexts, particularly women, the transformations now occurring are dramatic and shattering.

Heterosexuality, homosexuality

Rubin's research deals only with heterosexual activities. Her decision to exclude homosexual experiences is odd, given the fact, already revealed by Kinsey, that a very high proportion of men, as well as a substantial proportion of women, have taken part in homosexual acts at some time in their lives. Kinsey found that only about 50 per cent of all American men were, in his terms, 'exclusively heterosexual' – that is, had neither participated in homosexual activities, nor felt homosexual desires. Eighteen per cent were either exclusively homosexual or persistently bisexual. Among women, 2 per cent were wholly homosexual, 13 per cent of others had engaged in some form of homosexual activity, while a further 15 per cent reported having had homosexual urges without having acted on them.[7]

Kinsey's findings shocked a disbelieving public at the time. Over the past quarter of a century, however, homosexuality has been affected by changes as great as those influencing heterosexual conduct. Even at the date when the Kinsey volumes appeared, homosexuality was still seen in much of the clinical literature as a pathology, a form of psychosexual disturbance along with a whole range of others – fetishism, voyeurism, transvestism, satyriasis, nymphomania and so forth. It continues to be regarded as a perversion by many heterosexuals – that is, as specifically unnatural and to be morally condemned. Yet the term 'perversion' itself has now more or less completely disappeared from clinical psychiatry, and the aversion felt by many towards homosexuality no longer receives substantial support from the medical profession.

The 'coming out' of homosexuality is a very real process, with major consequences for sexual life in general. It was signalled by the popularising of the self-description 'gay', an example of that reflexive process whereby a social phenomenon can be appropriated and transformed through collective engagement. 'Gay', of course, suggests colourfulness, openness and legitimacy, a far cry from the image of homosexuality once held by many practising homosexuals as well as by the majority of heterosexual individuals. The gay cultural communities that came into being in American cities, as in many urban areas in Europe, provided a new public face for homosexuality. On a more personal level, however, the term 'gay' also brought with it an increasingly widespread reference to sexuality as a quality or property of the self. A person 'has' a sexuality, gay or otherwise, which can be reflexively grasped, interrogated and developed.

Sexuality thereby becomes free-floating; at the same time as 'gay' is something one can 'be', and 'discover oneself to be', sexuality opens itself up to many objects. Thus *The Kinsey Institute New Report on Sex*, published in 1990, describes a case of a 65-year-old man whose wife died following a happy marriage lasting for forty-five years. Within a year of his wife's death, he fell in love with a man. According to his own testimony, he had never before been sexually attracted to a man or fantasised about homosexual acts. Such an individual now follows his altered sexual orientation quite openly, although he has had to face the problem of 'what to tell the children'.[8] Would he even a few years ago have conceived of the possibility that he might transform his 'sexuality' in this way? He has entered a new world in much the same way as Graham did.

The idea of the 'relationship' emerges as strongly in gay sub-cultures as among the more heterosexual population. Male homosexuals commonly have a diversity of sexual partners, contact with whom may be only fleeting – as epitomised in the bath-house culture before the advent of AIDS led to its virtual disappearance. In a study undertaken in the late 1970s, some six hundred male homosexuals in the US were asked how many sexual partners they had had; about 40 per cent stated the number at five hundred or more.[9]

It might seem as though we find here a social universe of male sexuality run rampant, where one-night stands have become random ten-minute couplings. In fact, a high proportion of gay men, and the majority of lesbian women, are at any one time in a live-in relation with a partner. The same studies just quoted found that most people contacted had been in a relationship with one main partner at least once for a period of two years or more. Research undertaken by the Kinsey Institute in the early 1980s, based upon interviews with several hundred homosexual men, found that virtually all were at one point or another in a steady relationship for at least a year.[10] Gay women and men have preceded most heterosexuals in developing relationships, in the sense that term has come to assume today when applied to personal life. For they have had to 'get along' without traditionally established frameworks of marriage, in conditions of relative equality between partners.

'Sexuality' today has been discovered, opened up and made accessible to the development of varying life-styles. It is something each of us 'has', or cultivates, no longer a natural condition which an individual accepts as a preordained state of affairs. Somehow, in a way that has to be investigated, sexuality functions as a malleable feature of self, a prime connecting point between body, self-identity and social norms.

Such changes are nowhere better demonstrated than in the case of masturbation, once the dread symbol of failed sexuality. Masturbation has 'come out' as openly as homosexuality. The Kinsey Report found that 90 per cent of men, and 40 per cent of women, had at some time in their lives engaged in masturbation. Figures from more recent surveys have upped these proportions to almost 100 per cent in the case of men and around 70 per cent for women. Equally important: masturbation is widely recommended as a major source of sexual pleasure, and actively encouraged as a mode of improving sexual responsiveness on the part of both sexes.[11]

In what ways do the changes just discussed interact with transformations in personal life more generally? How do the changes of the past few decades connect to more protracted influences upon sexual conduct? To answer these questions means investigating how 'sexuality' originated, what it is and how it has come to be something that individuals 'possess'. These problems will be my concern in the book as a whole. But one particular work has dominated thinking about these issues in recent years, and we can make an initial approach to them through a brief critical appraisal of it: Michel Foucault's account of the history of sexuality.

To forestall possible misunderstandings, let me emphasise that a full-scale encounter with Foucault's thought would be out of place in this study, and I do not attempt such a thing. Foucault's brilliant innovations pose certain key issues in ways which no one had thought to do before. In my view, however, his writings are also deeply flawed, in respect both of the philosophical standpoint that he elaborates and some of the more historical claims he makes or implies. Admirers of Foucault will be unhappy: I don't justify these claims in any detail. My differences from Foucault, nevertheless, emerge clearly enough in the substance of the arguments I develop; I use his work mainly as a foil against which to clarify those arguments.

NOTES

1 All quotations are from Julian Barnes: *Before She Met Me*, London: Picador, 1986.
2 Lawrence Stone: *The Road to Divorce. England 1530–1987*, Oxford: Oxford University Press, 1990, p. 7.
3 Barnes: *Before She Met Me*, pp. 55ff.
4 Lillian Rubin: *Erotic Wars*, New York: Farrar, Straus and Giroux, 1990, p. 8.
5 Ibid., p. 61.
6 Ibid., p. 146.
7 Alfred C. Kinsey et al.: *Sexual Behaviour in the Human Male*, Philadelphia: Saunders, 1948; *Sexual Behaviour in the Human Female*, Philadelphia: Saunders, 1953.
8 June M. Reinisch and Ruth Beasley: *The Kinsey Institute New Report on Sex*, Harmondsworth: Penguin, 1990, p. 143.
9 Ibid., p. 144.
10 Ibid., p. 145.
11 W. H. Masters and V. E. Johnson: *Human Sexual Response*, Boston: Little, Brown, 1966.

2

FOUCAULT ON SEXUALITY

In *The History of Sexuality*, Foucault sets out to attack what, in a celebrated phrase, he calls 'the repressive hypothesis'.[1] According to such a view, modern institutions compel us to pay a price – increasing repression – for the benefits they offer. Civilisation means discipline, and discipline in turn implies control of inner drives, control that to be effective has to be internal. Who says modernity says super-ego. Foucault himself seemed to accept something of a similar view in his earlier writings, seeing modern social life as intrinsically bound up with the rise of 'disciplinary power', characteristic of the prison and the asylum, but also of other organisations, such as business firms, schools or hospitals. Disciplinary power supposedly produced 'docile bodies', controlled and regulated in their activities rather than able spontaneously to act on the promptings of desire.

Power here appeared above all as a constraining force. Yet as Foucault came to appreciate, power is a mobilising phenomenon, not just one which sets limits; and those who are subject to disciplinary power are not at all necessarily docile in their reactions to it. Power, therefore, can be an instrument for the production of pleasure: it does not only stand opposed to it. 'Sexuality' should not be understood only as a drive which social forces have to contain. Rather, it is 'an especially dense transfer point for relations of power', something which can be harnessed as a focus of social control through the very energy which, infused with power, it generates.

Sex is not driven underground in modern civilisation. On the contrary, it comes to be continually discussed and investigated. It has become part of 'a great sermon', replacing the more ancient tradition of theological preaching. Statements about sexual repression and the sermon of transcendence mutually reinforce one another; the struggle for sexual liberation is part of the self-same apparatus of power that it denounces. Has any other social order, Foucault asks rhetorically, been so persistently and pervasively preoccupied with sex?

The nineteenth and early twentieth centuries are Foucault's main concern in his encounter with the repressive hypothesis. During this period, sexuality and power became intertwined in several distinct ways. Sexuality was developed *as* a secret, which then had to be endlessly tracked down as well as guarded against. Take the case of masturbation. Whole campaigns were mounted by doctors and educators to lay siege to this dangerous phenomenon and make clear its consequences. So much attention was given to it, however, that we may suspect that the objective was not its elimination; the point was to organise the individual's development, bodily and mentally.

Such was also the case, Foucault continues, with the numerous perversions catalogued by psychiatrists, doctors and others. These diverse forms of aberrant sexuality were both opened to public display and made into principles of classification of individual conduct, personality and self-identity. The effect was not to suppress perversions, but to give them 'an analytical, visible, and permanent reality'; they were 'implanted in bodies, slipped in beneath modes of conduct'. Thus in pre-modern law, sodomy was defined as a prohibited act, but was not a quality or behaviour pattern of an individual. The nineteenth-century homosexual, however, became 'a personage, a past, a case history' as well as 'a type of life, a life form, a morphology'. 'We must not imagine', in Foucault's words,

> that all these things that were formerly tolerated attracted notice and received a pejorative designation when the time came to give a regulative role to the one type of sexuality that was capable of reproducing labour power and the form of the family . . . It is through the isolation, intensification, and consolidation of peripheral sexualities that the relations of power to sex and pleasure branched out and multiplied, measured the body, and penetrated modes of conduct.[2]

Many traditional cultures and civilisations have fostered arts of erotic sensibility; but only modern Western society has developed a science of sexuality. This has come about, in Foucault's view, through the conjoining of the principle of the confession to the accumulation of knowledge about sex.

Sex becomes in fact the focal point of a modern confessional. The Catholic confessional, Foucault points out, was always a means of regulating the sexual life of believers. It covered far more than only sexual indiscretions, and owning up to such misdemeanours was interpreted by priest and penitent alike in terms of a broad ethical framework. As part of the Counter-Reformation, the Church became more insistent upon regular confession, and the whole process was intensified. Not only acts, but thoughts, reveries and all details concerning sex were to be brought to view and scrutinised. The 'flesh' to which we are heir in Christian doctrine, which comes to include soul and body combined, was the proximate origin of that characteristic modern sexual preoccupation: sexual desire.

Somewhere in the late eighteenth century, confession as penitence became confession as interrogation. It was channelled into diverse discourses – from the case-history and

scientific treatise to scandalous tracts such as the anonymous *My Secret Life*. Sex is a 'secret' created by texts which
abjure as well as those which celebrate it. Access to this
secret is believed to disclose 'truth': sexuality is fundamental
to the 'regime of truth' characteristic of modernity. Confession in its modern sense 'is all those procedures by which
the subject is incited to produce a discourse of truth about
his sexuality which is capable of having effects on the subject
himself'.[3]

Teams of experts, sexologists and assorted specialists
thence stand ready to delve into the secret they have helped
to create. Sex is endowed with vast causal powers, and
seems to have an influence over many diverse actions.[4] The
very effort poured into investigation turns sex into something clandestine, ever resistant to easy observation. Like
madness, sexuality is not a phenomenon which already
exists, awaiting rational analysis and therapeutic correction.
Erotic pleasure becomes 'sexuality' as its investigation produces texts, manuals and surveys which distinguish 'normal
sexuality' from its pathological domains. The truth and the
secret of sex were each established by the pursuit and the
making available of such 'findings'.

The study of sex and the creation of discourses about it
led in the nineteenth century to the development of various
contexts of power-knowledge. One concerned women.
Female sexuality was recognised and immediately crushed
– treated as the pathological origin of hysteria. Another was
to do with children; the 'finding' that children are sexually
active was tied to the declaration that the sexuality of
children was 'contrary to nature'. A further context concerned marriage and the family. Sex in marriage was to be
responsible and self-regulated; not just confined to marriage, but ordered in distinct and specific ways. Contraception was discouraged. Control of family size was supposed
to emerge spontaneously from the disciplined pursuit of

pleasure. Finally, a catalogue of perversions was introduced and modes of treatment for them described.

The invention of sexuality, for Foucault, was part of certain distinct processes involved in the formation and consolidation of modern social institutions. Modern states, and modern organisations, depend upon the meticulous control of populations across time and space. Such control was generated by the development of an 'anatamo-politics of the human body' – technologies of bodily management aimed at regulating, but also optimising, the capabilities of the body. 'Anatamo-politics' is in turn one focus of a more broadly based realm of biopower.[5]

The study of sex, Foucault remarks in an interview, is boring. After all, why spin out yet another discourse to add to the multiplicity which already exist? What is interesting is the emergence of an 'apparatus of sexuality', a 'positive economy of the body and pleasure'.[6] Foucault came to concentrate more and more upon this 'apparatus' in relation to the self and his studies of sex in the Classical world help illuminate the issue as he sees it.[7] The Greeks were concerned to foster the 'care of the self', but in a way that was 'diametrically opposed' to the development of the self in the modern social order, which in its extreme guise he sometimes labels the 'Californian cult of the self'. In between these two, again, was the influence of Christianity. In the Ancient world, among the upper class at least, the care of the self was integrated into an ethics of the cultivated, aesthetic existence. To the Greeks, Foucault tells us, food and diet were much more important than sex. Christianity substituted for the Classical view the idea of a self which has to be renounced: the self is something to be deciphered, its truth identified. In the 'Californian cult of the self', 'one is supposed to discover one's true self, to separate it from what might obscure or alienate it, to decipher its truth thanks to psychological or psychoanalytic science'.[8]

Sexuality and institutional change

'Sexuality', as Foucault says, is indeed a term which appears for the first time in the nineteenth century. The word existed in the technical jargon of biology and zoology as early as 1800, but only towards the end of the century did it come to be used widely in something close to the meaning it has for us today – as what the *Oxford English Dictionary* refers to as 'the quality of being sexual or having sex'. The word appears in this sense in a book published in 1889 that was concerned with why women are prone to various illnesses from which men are exempt – something accounted for by women's 'sexuality'.[9] That it was originally connected with attempts to keep feminine sexual activity in check is amply demonstrated in the literature of the era. Sexuality emerged as a source of worry, needing solutions; women who crave sexual pleasure are specifically unnatural. As one medical specialist wrote, 'what is the habitual condition of the man [sexual excitation] is the exception with the woman'.[10]

Sexuality is a social construct, operating within fields of power, not merely a set of biological promptings which either do or do not find direct release. Yet we cannot accept Foucault's thesis that there is more or less a straightforward path of development from a Victorian 'fascination' with sexuality through to more recent times.[11] There are major contrasts between sexuality as disclosed through Victorian medical literature, and effectively marginalised there, and sexuality as an everyday phenomenon of thousands of books, articles and other descriptive sources today. Moreover, the repressions of the Victorian era and after were in some respects all too real, as generations of women above all can attest.[12]

It is difficult, if not impossible, to make sense of these issues if we stay within the overall theoretical position that Foucault developed, in which the only moving forces are power, discourse and the body. Power moves in mysterious ways in Foucault's writings, and history, as the actively made achievement of human subjects, scarcely exists. Let us therefore accept his arguments about the social origins of sexuality but set them in a different interpretative framework. Foucault puts too much emphasis upon sexuality at the expense of gender. He is silent about the connections of sexuality with romantic love, a phenomenon closely bound up with changes in the family. Moreover, his discussion of the nature of sexuality largely remains at the level of discourse – and rather specific forms of discourse at that. Finally, one must place in question his conception of the self in relation to modernity.

Foucault argues that sexuality in Victorian times was a secret, but an open secret, ceaselessly discussed in different texts and medical sources. The phenomenon of variegated medical debate is important, much for the reasons he gives. Yet it would plainly be a mistake to suppose that sex was widely represented, analysed or surveyed in sources available to the mass of the public. Medical journals and other semi-official publications were accessible only to very few; and until the latter part of the nineteenth century most of the population were not even literate. The confining of sexuality *to* technical arenas of discussion was a mode of *de facto* censorship; this literature was not available to the majority, even of the educated population. Such censorship tangibly affected women more than men. Many women married having virtually no knowledge about sex at all, save that it was to do with the undesirable urges of men, and had to be endured. A mother famously thus says to her daughter, 'After your wedding my dear, unpleasant things will happen to you but take no notice of them, I never did.'[13]

Here is Amber Hollibaugh, a lesbian activist, calling in the 1980s for a 'speak out' for women that will publicly reveal yearnings not yet fully articulated:

Where are all the women who don't come gently and don't want to; don't know what they like but intend to find out; are the lovers of butch or feminine women; who like fucking men; practise consensual S/M; feel more like faggots than dykes; love dildos, penetration, costumes; like to sweat, talk dirty, see expression of need sweep across their lovers' faces; are confused and need to experiment with their own tentative ideas of passion; think gay male pash is hot?[14]

The fascination with sex that Foucault notes is plainly there in Hollibaugh's ecstatic exhortation; but, on the face of things at least, could anything be more different from the tedious, male-authored medical texts he describes? How have we got from one point to the other over a period of little more than a century?

If we followed Foucault, the answers to these questions would seem rather easy. The Victorian obsession with sex, it could be argued, was eventually brought to a culmination by Freud, who, beginning from a puzzlement about hysterical women, came to see sexuality as the core of all human experience. At about the same juncture, Havelock Ellis and the other sexologists set to work, declaring the pursuit of sexual pleasure on the part of both sexes to be desirable and necessary. From there it is just a few short steps via Kinsey, and Masters and Johnson, to a work such as *Treat Yourself to Sex*, in which the reader is compared sexually to a radio receiver: 'Ask yourself why you have stopped fiddling with the reception. How often have you enjoyed an unexpected programme which you came upon by chance when playing with the knobs?'[15]

Yet things are not so simple. To explain how such changes have come about, we have to move away from an overwhelming emphasis on discourse, and look to factors largely absent from Foucault's analysis. Some concern quite long-term influences, while others are confined to a more recent period.

The long-term trends I shall indicate only briefly, although their overall importance is fundamental since they set the stage for those affecting the later phase. During the nineteenth century, the formation of marriage ties, for most groups in the population, became based on considerations other than judgements of economic value. Notions of romantic love, first of all having their main hold over bourgeois groups, were diffused through much of the social order. 'Romancing' became a synonym for courting, and 'romances' were the first form of literature to reach a mass population. The spread of ideals of romantic love was one factor tending to disentangle the marital bond from wider kinship ties and give it an especial significance. Husbands and wives increasingly became seen as collaborators in a joint emotional enterprise, this having primacy even over their obligations towards their children. The 'home' came into being as a distinct environment set off from work; and, at least in principle, became a place where individuals could expect emotional support, as contrasted with the instrumental character of the work setting. Particularly important for its implications for sexuality, pressures to have large families, characteristic of virtually all pre-modern cultures, gave way to a tendency to limit family size in a rigorous way. Such practice, seemingly an innocent demographic statistic, placed a finger on the historical trigger so far as sexuality was concerned. For the first time, for a mass population of women, sexuality could become separated from a chronic round of pregnancy and childbirth.

The contraction in family size was historically a condition as much as a consequence of the introduction of modern methods of contraception. Birth control, of course, long had its advocates, most of them women, but the family planning movement did not have a widespread influence in most countries until after World War I. A change in official opinion in the UK, until that date often vehemently hostile, was signalled when Lord Dawson, physician to the King, reluctantly declared in a speech to the Church in 1921: 'Birth control is here to stay. It is an established fact and, for good or evil, has to be accepted . . . No denunciations will abolish it.' His view still upset many. The *Sunday Express* declared in response, 'Lord Dawson must go!'[16]

Effective contraception meant more than an increased capability of limiting pregnancy. In combination with the other influences affecting family size noted above, it signalled a deep transition in personal life. For women – and, in a partly different sense, for men also – sexuality became malleable, open to being shaped in diverse ways, and a potential 'property' of the individual.

Sexuality came into being as part of a progressive differentiation of sex from the exigencies of reproduction. With the further elaboration of reproductive technologies, that differentiation has today become complete. Now that conception can be artificially produced, rather than only artificially inhibited, sexuality is at last fully autonomous. Reproduction can occur in the absence of sexual activity; this is a final 'liberation' for sexuality, which thence can become wholly a quality of individuals and their transactions with one another.

The creation of *plastic sexuality*, severed from its age-old integration with reproduction, kinship and the generations, was the precondition of the sexual revolution of the past several decades. For most women, in most cultures, and throughout most periods of history, sexual pleasure, where possible, was intrinsically bound up with fear – of repetitive pregnancies, and therefore of death, given the substantial proportion of women who perished in childbirth and the very high rates of infant mortality which prevailed. The breaking of these connections was thus a phenomenon with truly radical implications. AIDS, one might say, has reintroduced the connection of sexuality to death, but this is not a reversion to the old situation, because AIDS does not distinguish between the sexes.

The 'sexual revolution' of the past thirty or forty years is not just, or even primarily, a gender-neutral advance in sexual permissiveness. It involves two basic elements. One is a revolution in female sexual autonomy – concentrated in that period, but having antecedents stretching back to the nineteenth century.[17] Its consequences for male sexuality are profound and it is very much of an unfinished revolution. The second element is the flourishing of homosexuality, male and female. Homosexuals of both sexes have staked out new sexual ground well in advance of the more sexually 'orthodox'. Each of these developments has something to do with the sexual libertarianism proclaimed by the social movements of the 1960s, but the contribution of such libertarianism to the emergence of plastic sexuality was neither necessary nor particularly direct. We are dealing here with much more deep-lying, and irreversible, changes than were brought about by such movements, important although they were in facilitating more unfettered discussion of sexuality than previously was possible.

Institutional reflexivity and sexuality

In analysing sexual development, Foucault is surely right to argue that discourse becomes constitutive of the social reality it portrays. Once there is a new terminology for understanding sexuality, ideas, concepts and theories couched in these terms seep into social life itself, and help reorder it. For Foucault, however, this process appears as a fixed and one-way intrusion of 'power-knowledge' into social organisation. Without denying its connectedness to power, we should see the phenomenon rather as one of *institutional reflexivity* and as constantly in motion. It is institutional, because it is a basic structuring element of social activity in modern settings. It is reflexive in the sense that terms introduced to describe social life routinely enter and transform it – not as a mechanical process, nor necessarily in a controlled way, but because they become part of the frames of action which individuals or groups adopt.

An expansion of institutional reflexivity is a distinctive characteristic of modern societies in the relatively recent period. Increased geographical mobility, the mass media and a host of other factors have undercut elements of tradition in social life which long resisted – or became adapted to – modernity. The continual reflexive incorporation of knowledge not only steps into the breach; it provides precisely a basic impetus to the changes which sweep through personal, as well as global, contexts of action. In the area of sexual discourse, more far-reaching in their effects than the openly propagandist texts advising on the search for sexual pleasure are those reporting on, analysing and commenting about sexuality in practice. The Kinsey Reports, like others following on, aimed to analyse what was going on in a particular region of social activity, as all social research seeks to do. Yet as they disclosed, they also influenced, initiating cycles of debate, reinvestigation and further debate. These debates became part of a wide public domain, but also served to alter lay views of sexual actions and involvements themselves. No doubt the 'scientific' cast of such investigations helps neutralise moral uneasiness about the propriety of particular sexual practices. Far more importantly, however, the rise of such researches signals, and contributes to, an accelerating reflexivity on the level of ordinary, everyday sexual practices.

In my opinion, all this has little to do with the confessional, even in the very general sense of that term used by Foucault. Foucault's discussion of this topic, thought-provoking though it is, simply seems mistaken. Therapy and counselling, including psychoanalysis, we may agree, become increasingly prominent with the maturation of modern societies. Their centrality, though, is not a result of the fact that, as Foucault puts it, they provide 'regulated procedures for the confession of sex'.[18] Even if we consider only psychoanalysis, comparison with the confessional is too forced to be convincing. In the confessional it is assumed that the individual is readily able to provide the information required. Psychoanalysis, however, supposes that emotional blockages, deriving from the past, inhibit an individual's self-understanding and autonomy of action.[19]

Foucault's interpretation of the development of the self in modern societies should also be placed in question in a rather basic way. Instead of seeing the self as constructed by a specific 'technology', we should recognise that self-identity becomes particularly problematic in modern social life, particularly in the very recent era. Fundamental features of a society of high reflexivity are the 'open' character of self-identity and the reflexive nature of the body. For women struggling to break free from pre-existing gender roles, the question 'Who am I?' – which Betty Frieden labelled 'the problem that has no name'[20] – comes to the surface with particular intensity. Much the same is true for homosexuals, male and female, who contest dominant heterosexual stereotypes. The question is one of sexual identity, but not only this. The self today is for everyone a reflexive project – a more or less continuous interrogation of past, present and future.[21] It is a project carried on amid a profusion of reflexive resources: therapy and self-help manuals of all kinds, television programmes and magazine articles.

Against this backdrop, we can interpret Freud's contribution to modern culture in a different light from Foucault. The importance of Freud was not that he gave the modern preoccupation with sex its most cogent formulation. Rather, Freud disclosed the connections between sexuality and self-identity when they were still entirely obscure and at the same time showed those connections to be problematic. Psychoanalysis has its origins in the medical treatment of behaviour pathologies, and was seen by Freud as a method of combating neurosis. It is understood in this light by many of its practitioners to this day, as are most other forms of therapy it has helped to inspire. Psychoanalysis may cure neuroses – although its success in this respect is debatable. Its specific significance, however, is that it provides a setting, and a rich fund of theoretical and conceptual resources, for the creation of a reflexively ordered narrative of self. In a therapeutic situation, whether of a classical psychoanalytic type or not, individuals are able (in principle) to bring their past 'into line' with exigencies of the present, consolidating an emotional story-line with which they feel relatively content.

What applies to self applies to body. The body, plainly enough, is in some sense – yet to be determined – the domain of sexuality. Like sexuality, and the self, it is today heavily infused with reflexivity. The body has always been adorned, cosseted and, sometimes, in the pursuit of higher ideals, mutilated or starved. What explains, however, our distinctive concerns with bodily appearance and control today, which differ in certain obvious ways from those more traditional preoccupations? Foucault has an answer, and it is one which brings in sexuality. Modern societies, he says, in specific contrast to the pre-modern world, depend upon the generating of biopower. Yet this is at most a half-truth. The body becomes a focus of administrative power, to be sure. But, more than this, it becomes a visible carrier of self-identity and is increasingly integrated into life-style decisions which an individual makes.

The reflexivity of the body accelerates in a fundamental way with the invention of diet in its modern meaning – different, of course, from the Ancient one – something that, as a mass phenomenon, dates from no earlier than several decades ago. Diet is linked to the introduction of a 'science' of nutrition, and thus to administrative power in Foucault's sense; but it also places responsibility for the development and appearance of the body squarely in the hands of its possessor. What an individual eats, even among the more materially deprived, becomes a reflexively infused question of dietary selection. *Everyone* today in the developed countries, apart from the very poor, is 'on a diet'. With the increased efficiency of global markets, not only is food abundant, but a diversity of foodstuffs is available for the consumer all year round. In these circumstances, what one eats is a life-style choice, influenced by, and constructed through, vast numbers of cookbooks, popular medical tracts, nutritional guides and so forth. Is it any wonder that eating disorders have replaced hysteria as the pathologies of our age? Is it any wonder that such disorders mostly affect women, particularly young women? For diet connects physical appearance, self-identity and sexuality in the context of social changes with which individuals struggle to cope. Emaciated bodies today no longer bear witness to ecstatic devotion, but to the intensity of this secular battle.

The decline of perversion

What, though, should we make of the decline of 'perversion'? How can it be that sexual actions that once were so severely condemned, and sometimes remain formally illegal, are now very widely practised, and in many circles actively fostered? Once more, it is fairly easy to trace out the surface story. The sexologists, as well as Freud and at least some of his more heterodox followers, largely subverted the moral overtones of the notion of perversion. Freud's much-debated *Three Essays on the Theory of Sexuality*, first published in 1905, sought to demonstrate that the sexual traits associated with perversions, far from being restricted to small categories of abnormal people, are qualities common to the sexuality of everyone. Hence, Freud concluded, it is 'inappropriate to use the word perversion as a term of reproach'.[22] Havelock Ellis similarly declared the term unacceptable, substituting for it 'sexual deviation'.

At a subsequent date, it might be argued, interest groups and movements began actively claiming social acceptance and legal legitimacy for homosexuality, contesting even the terminology of deviation. Thus, for example, in the US groups such as the Mattachine Society and the Daughters of Bilitis were set up as the high tide of McCarthyism receded. The subsequent creation of large gay communities provided for an efflorescence of new groups and associations, many promoting minority sexual tastes. The battle to secure public tolerance for homosexuality led other organisations concerned with promoting sexual pluralism to 'come out'. As Jeffrey Weeks puts it:

> There no longer appears to be a great continent of normality surrounded by small islands of disorder. Instead we can now witness clusters of islands, great and small . . . New categories and erotic minorities have emerged. Older ones have experienced a process of subdivision as specialised tastes, specific aptitudes and needs become the basis for proliferating sexual identities.[23]

Expressed in another way, sexual diversity, although still regarded by many hostile groups as perversion, has moved out of Freud's case-history notebooks into the everyday social world.

Seen in these terms, the decline of perversion can be understood as a partly successful battle over rights of self-expression in the context of the liberal democratic state. Victories have been won, but the confrontations continue, and freedoms that have been achieved could still plausibly be swept away on a reactionary tide. Homosexuals still face deeply entrenched prejudice and, quite commonly, open violence. Their emancipatory struggles encounter resistances perhaps as deep as those that continue to obstruct women's access to social and economic equality.

There is no reason to doubt such an interpretation. Yet there is again another way of looking at things, which suggests that the incipient replacement of perversion by pluralism is part of a broad-based set of changes integral to the expansion of modernity. Modernity is associated with the socialisation of the natural world – the progressive replacement of structures and events that were external parameters of human activity by socially organised processes. Not only social life itself, but what used to be 'nature' becomes dominated by socially organised systems.[24] Reproduction was once part of nature, and heterosexual activity was inevitably its focal point. Once sexuality has become an 'integral' component of social relations, as a result of changes already discussed, heterosexuality is no longer a standard by which everything else is judged. We have not yet reached a stage in which heterosexuality is accepted as only one taste among others, but such is the implication of the socialisation of reproduction.

This view of the decline of perversion is not inconsistent with the other view, for tolerance always has to be fought for in the public domain. It provides, however, a more structural interpretation of the phenomenon, an interpretation in which the emergence of plastic sexuality has a prime place. I shall have a good deal more to say about plastic sexuality in what follows. But first of all I turn to what Foucault specifically neglects: the nature of love and, in particular, the rise of ideals of romantic love. The transmutation of love is as much a phenomenon of modernity as is the emergence of sexuality; and it connects in an immediate way with issues of reflexivity and self-identity.

NOTES

1 *The History of Sexuality* is in three volumes, of which vol. 1: *An Introduction*, Harmondsworth: Pelican, 1981, is by far the most relevant here.
2 Ibid., pp. 47–8.
3 Michel Foucault: 'The confession of the flesh', in Colin Gordon: *Michel Foucault: Power/Knowledge*, Hemel Hempstead: Harvester, 1980, pp. 215–16.
4 Michel Foucault: 'Technologies of the self', in Luther H. Martin et al.: *Technologies of the Self*, London: Tavistock, 1988. 'Unlike other interdictions, sexual interdictions are constantly connected with the obligation to tell the truth about oneself' (p. 16).
5 Foucault: *The History of Sexuality*, vol. 1, p. 142.
6 Foucault: 'The confession of the flesh'.
7 Michel Foucault: Preface to *The History of Sexuality*, vol. 2: *The Use of Pleasure*, Harmondsworth: Penguin, 1987.
8 Michel Foucault: 'On the genealogy of ethics: an overview of work in progress', in Paul Rabinow: *The Foucault Reader*, Harmondsworth: Penguin, 1986, p. 362. For the best secondary discussion of Foucault and the self, see Lois McNay: *Foucault and Feminism*, Cambridge: Polity, 1992.
9 Stephen Heath: *The Sexual Fix*, London: Macmillan, 1982, pp. 7–16.
10 Quoted in ibid., p. 17.
11 For one version of such a view, see Heath, *The Sexual Fix*.
12 Lawrence Stone: 'Passionate attachments in the West in historical perspective', in William Gaylin and Ethel Person: *Passionate Attachments*, New York: Free Press, 1988. There have been many discussions of the 'repressive hypothesis'. See, for example, Peter Gay: *The Bourgeois Experience*, Oxford: Oxford University Press, vol. 1, 1984; vol. 2, 1986. Cf. also James MaHood and Kristine Wenburg: *The Mosher Survey*, New York: Arno, 1980, which concerns a study of forty-five Victorian women, carried out by Celia Mosher. Thirty-four per cent of her respondents said they 'always' or 'usually' experienced orgasm in sexual relations, a rate which compares favourably with the Kinsey Report on women. The extraordinary work by Ronald Hyam: *Empire and Sexuality*, Manchester: Manchester University Press, 1990, demonstrates

that 'Victorianism' cannot be understood if limited to Britain. 'Repression' at home went along with widespread sexual licence in the imperial domains – on the part of the male colonisers.

13 Quoted in Carol Adams: *Ordinary Lives*, London: Virago, 1982, p. 129.
14 Amber Hollibaugh: 'Desire for the future: radical hope in passion and pleasure', in Carole S. Vance: *Pleasure and Danger. Exploring Female Sexuality*, London: Routledge, 1984, p. 403.
15 Paul Brown and Carolyn Faulder: *Treat Yourself to Sex*, Harmondsworth: Penguin, 1979, p. 35.
16 Quoted in Adams: *Ordinary Lives*, p. 138.
17 This point is developed in some detail in Barbara Ehrenreich et al.: *Re-making Love*, London: Fontana, 1987.
18 Foucault: 'The confession of the flesh'.
19 Jacques-Alain Miller, contribution to Foucault: 'The confession of the flesh'. See also Mark Cousins and Athar Hussain: *Michel Foucault*, London: Macmillan, 1984, pp. 212–15.
20 Betty Frieden: *The Feminine Mystique*, Harmondsworth: Penguin, 1965.
21 Anthony Giddens: *Modernity and Self-Identity*, Cambridge: Polity, 1991.
22 Sigmund Freud: 'The sexual aberrations', in *Three Essays on the Theory of Sexuality*, Standard Edition, London: Hogarth, 1953, p. 160.
23 Jeffrey Weeks: *Sexuality*, London: Tavistock, 1986, ch. 4.
24 Giddens: *Modernity and Self-Identity*.

3

ROMANTIC LOVE AND OTHER ATTACHMENTS

'Love', Bronislaw Malinowski observes in his study of the Trobriand Islanders, 'is a passion to the Melanesian as to the European, and torments mind and body to a greater or lesser extent; it leads to many an *impasse*, scandal, or tragedy; more rarely, it illuminates life and makes the heart expand and overflow with joy.'[1] Numerous examples of love poetry survive among the relics of Ancient Egypt, some dating back from more than 1000 BC. Love is there portrayed as overwhelming the ego, and thus akin to a kind of sickness, although also having healing powers:

> The sight of her makes me well!
> When she opens her eyes my body is young,
> Her speaking makes me strong;
> Embracing her expels my malady –
> Seven days since she went from me![2]

While the secular use of the word 'passion' – as distinct from its older usage, meaning religious passion – is relatively modern, it makes sense to regard passionate love, *amour passion*,[3] as expressing a generic connection between love and sexual attachment. Passionate love is marked by an urgency which sets it apart from the routines of everyday life with which, indeed, it tends to come into conflict. The emotional involvement with the other is pervasive – so strong that it may lead the individual, or both individuals, to ignore their ordinary obligations. Passionate love has a quality of enchantment which can be religious in its fervour. Everything in the world seems suddenly fresh, yet perhaps at the same time fails to capture the individual's interest, which is so strongly bound up with the love object. On the level of personal relations, passionate love is specifically disruptive in a similar sense to charisma; it uproots the individual from the mundane and generates a preparedness to consider radical options as well as sacrifices.[4] For this reason, seen from the point of view of social order and duty, it is dangerous. It is hardly surprising that passionate love has nowhere been recognised as either a necessary or sufficient basis for marriage, and in most cultures has been seen as refractory to it.

Passionate love is a more or less universal phenomenon. It should be differentiated, I shall argue, from romantic love, which is much more culturally specific. In what follows I shall try to identify certain distinctive features of romantic love and pursue their implications. My purpose is primarily analytic; I am not concerned to write a history of romantic love, even in miniature. However, to begin with, a very brief historical interpretation is needed.

Marriage, sexuality and romantic love

In pre-modern Europe, most marriages were contracted, not on the basis of mutual sexual attraction, but economic circumstance. Among the poor marriage was a means of organising agrarian labour. A life characterised by unremitting hard labour was unlikely to be conducive to sexual passion. It has been claimed that among the peasantry in seventeenth-century France and Germany, kissing, caressing and other forms of physical affection associated with sex were rare among married couples. Opportunities for men to engage in extramarital liaisons, however, were often quite numerous.[5]

Only among aristocratic groups was sexual licence openly permitted among 'respectable' women. Sexual freedom follows power and is an expression of it; at certain times and places, in aristocratic strata, women were sufficiently liberated from the demands of reproduction, and from routine work, to be able to pursue their independent sexual pleasure. Of course, this was virtually never connected with marriage. Most civilisations seem to have created stories and myths which drive home the message that those who seek to create permanent attachments through passionate love are doomed.

The differentiation drawn between the 'chaste' sexuality of marriage and the erotic or passionate character of extramarital affairs was quite common among other aristocracies besides those of Europe. Specific to Europe was the emergence of ideals of love closely connected to the moral values of Christianity.[6] The precept that one should devote oneself to God in order to know him, and that through this process self-knowledge is achieved, became part of a mystical unity between man and woman. The temporary idealisation of the other typical of passionate love here was joined to a more permanent involvement with the love object; and a certain reflexivity was already present even at an early date.[7]

Romantic love, which began to make its presence felt from the late eighteenth century onwards, drew upon such ideals and incorporated elements of *amour passion*, while nevertheless becoming distinct from both. Romantic love introduced the idea of a narrative into an individual's life – a formula which radically extended the reflexivity of sublime love. The telling of a story is one of the meanings of 'romance', but this story now became individualised, inserting self and other into a personal narrative which had no particular reference to wider social processes. The rise of romantic love more or less coincided with the emergence of the novel: the connection was one of newly discovered narrative form.

The complex of ideas associated with romantic love for the first time associated love with freedom, both being seen as normatively desirable states. Passionate love has always been liberating, but only in the sense of generating a break with routine and duty. It was precisely this quality of *amour passion* which set it apart from existing institutions. Ideals of romantic love, by contrast, inserted themselves directly into the emergent ties between freedom and self-realisation.

In romantic love attachments, the element of sublime love tends to predominate over that of sexual ardour. The importance of this point can hardly be overstressed. The romantic love complex is in this respect as historically unusual as traits Max Weber found combined in the protestant ethic.[8] Love breaks with sexuality while embracing it; 'virtue' begins to take on a new sense for both sexes, no longer meaning only innocence but qualities of character which pick out the other person as 'special'.

Romantic love is often thought of as implying instantaneous attraction – 'love at first sight'. In so far as immediate attraction is part of romantic love, however, it has to be separated quite sharply from the sexual/erotic compulsions of passionate love. The 'first glance' is a communicative gesture, an intuitive grasp of qualities of the other. It is a process of attraction to someone who can make one's life, as it is said, 'complete'.

The idea of 'romance', in the sense which the term came to assume in the nineteenth century, both expressed and contributed to secular changes affecting social life as a whole.[9] Modernity is inseparable from the ascendancy of reason, in the sense that rational understanding of physical and social processes is supposed to replace the arbitrary rule of mysticism and dogma. Reason has no place for emotion, which simply lies outside its domain; but in fact emotional life became reordered in the changing conditions of day-to-day activities. Up to the threshold of the modern age, love charms, philtres and aphrodisiacs were the stock in trade of 'cunning' men and women, who could be turned to in order to help control the vagaries of sexual involvements. Alternatively, the priest could be consulted. The fate of the individual, however, in personal attachments as in other spheres, was tied to a broader cosmic order. 'Romance', as understood from the eighteenth century onwards, still had resonances of prior conceptions of cosmic fate, but mixed these with an attitude that looked to an open future. A romance was no longer, as it generally had been before, a specifically unreal conjuring of possibilities in a realm of fiction. Instead, it became a potential avenue for controlling the future, as well as a form of psychological security (in principle) for those whose lives were touched by it.

Gender and love

Some have said that romantic love was a plot engineered by men against women, in order to fill their minds with idle and impossible dreams. Yet such a view cannot explain the appeal of romantic literature, or the fact that women played a large part in its diffusion. 'There is scarce a young lady in the kingdom', a writer in The Lady's Magazine observed, with some hyperbole, in 1773, 'who has not read with avidity a great number of romances and novels.' These publications, the writer went on to add sourly, 'tend to vitiate the taste'.[10] An increasing tide of romantic novels and stories, which has not abated to this day – many written by women – flooded the bookstores from the early nineteenth century onwards.

The rise of the romantic love complex has to be understood in relation to several sets of influences which affected women from about the late eighteenth century onwards. One was the creation of the home, already referred to. A second was the changing relations between parents and children; a third was what some have termed the 'invention of motherhood'. So far as the status of women was concerned, all of these were quite closely integrated.[11]

Whether or not childhood itself is a creation of the relatively recent past, as Ariès has so famously claimed, it is beyond dispute that patterns of parent–child interaction altered substantially, for all classes, during the 'repressive' Victorian period. The strictness of the Victorian father is legendary. Yet in some respects patriarchal power in the domestic milieu was on the wane by the latter part of the nineteenth century. For the direct rule of the male over the household, comprehensive in nature when it was still the centre of a production system, became weakened with the separation of the home and the workplace. The husband held ultimate power, to be sure, but a growing emphasis upon the importance of emotional warmth between parents and children frequently softened his use of it. Women's control over child-rearing grew as families became smaller and children came to be identified as vulnerable and in need of long-term emotional training. As Mary Ryan has put it, the centre of the household moved 'from patriarchal authority to maternal affection'.[12]

Idealisation of the mother was one strand in the modern construction of motherhood, and undoubtedly fed directly into some of the values propagated about romantic love. The image of 'wife and mother' reinforced a 'two sex' model of activities and feelings. Women were recognised by men to be different, unknowable – concerned with a particular domain alien to men. The idea that each sex is a mystery to the other is an old one, and has been represented in various ways in different cultures. The distinctively novel element here was the association of motherhood with femininity as qualities of the personality – qualities which certainly infused widely held conceptions of female sexuality. As an article on marriage published in 1839 observed, 'the man bears rule over his wife's person and conduct. She bears the rule of his inclinations: he governs by law; she by persuasion . . . The empire of the woman is an empire of softness . . . her commands are caresses, her menaces are tears.'[13]

Romantic love was essentially feminised love. As Francesca Cancian has shown, prior to the late eighteenth century, if love was spoken about at all in relation to marriage, it was as companionate love, linked to the mutual responsibility of husbands and wives for running the household or farm. Thus in *The Well-Ordered Family*, which appeared just after the turn of the century, Benjamin Wadsworth wrote of the married couple that 'the duty of love is mutual, it should be performed by each to each'.[14] With the division of spheres, however, the fostering of love became predominantly the task of women. Ideas about romantic love were plainly allied to women's subordination in the home, and her relative separation from the outside world. But the development of such ideas was also an expression of women's power, a contradictory assertion of autonomy in the face of deprivation.

For men the tensions between romantic love and *amour passion* were dealt with by separating the comfort of the domestic environment from the sexuality of the mistress or whore. Male cynicism towards romantic love was readily bolstered by this division, which none the less implicitly accepted the feminisation of 'respectable' love. The prevalence of the double standard gave women no such outlet. Yet the fusion of ideals of romantic love and motherhood did allow women to develop new domains of intimacy. During the Victorian period, male friendship lost much of the quality of mutual involvement that comrades held for one another. Feelings of male comradeship were largely relegated to marginal activities, like sport or other leisure pursuits, or participation in war. For many women, things moved in the opposite direction. As specialists of the heart, women met each other on a basis of personal and social equality, within the broad spectra of class divisions. Friendships between women helped mitigate the disappointments of marriage, but also proved rewarding in their own right. Women spoke of friendships, as men often did, in terms of love; and they found there a true confessional.[15]

Avid consumption of romantic novels and stories was in one sense a testimony to passivity. The individual sought in fantasy what was denied in the ordinary world. The unreality of romantic stories from this angle was an expression of weakness, an inability to come to terms with frustrated self-identity in actual social life. Yet romantic literature was also (and is today) a literature of hope, a sort of refusal. It often rejected the idea of settled domesticity as the only salient ideal. In many romantic stories, after a flirtation with other types of men, the heroine discovers the virtues of the solid, reliable individual who makes a dependable husband. At least as often, however, the true hero is a flamboyant adventurer, distinguished by his exotic characteristics, who ignores convention in the pursuit of an errant life.

Let me sum up to this point. Romantic love became distinct from *amour passion*, although at the same time had residues of it. *Amour passion* was never a generic social force in the way in which romantic love has been from somewhere in the late eighteenth century up to relatively recent times. Together with other social changes, the spread of notions of romantic love was deeply involved with momentous transitions affecting marriage as well as other contexts of personal life. Romantic love presumes some degree of self-interrogation. How do I feel about the other? How does the other feel about me? Are our feelings 'profound' enough to support a long-term involvement? Unlike *amour passion*, which uproots erratically, romantic love detaches individuals from wider social circumstances in a different way. It provides for a long-term life trajectory, oriented to an anticipated yet malleable future; and it creates a 'shared history' that helps separate out the marital relationship from other aspects of family organisation and give it a special primacy.

From its earliest origins, romantic love raises the question of intimacy. It is incompatible with lust, and with earthy sexuality, not so much because the loved one is idealised – although this is part of the story – but because it presumes a psychic communication, a meeting of souls which is reparative in character. The other, by being who he or she is, answers a lack which the individual does not even necessarily recognise – until the love relation is initiated. And this lack is directly to do with self-identity: in some sense, the flawed individual is made whole.

Romantic love made of *amour passion* a specific cluster of beliefs and ideals geared to transcendence; romantic love may end in tragedy, and feed upon transgression, but it also produces triumph, a conquest of mundane prescriptions and compromises. Such love projects in two senses: it fastens upon and idealises another, and it projects a course of future development. Although most authors have concentrated on the first of these traits, the second is at least equally as important and in a sense underlies it. The dream-like, fantasy character of romance, as described in the popular literature of the nineteenth century, drew scorn from rationalist critics, male and female, who saw in it an absurd or pathetic escapism. In the view suggested here, however, romance is the counterfactual thinking of the deprived – and in the nineteenth century and thereafter participated in a major reworking of the conditions of personal life.

In romantic love, the absorption by the other typical of *amour passion* is integrated into the characteristic orientation of 'the quest'. The quest is an odyssey, in which self-identity awaits its validation from the discovery of the other. It has an active character, and in this respect modern romance contrasts with medieval romantic tales, in which the heroine usually is relatively passive. The women in modern romantic novels are mostly independent and spirited, and have consistently been portrayed in this way.[16] The conquest motif in these stories is not like the male version of sexual conquest: the heroine meets and melts the heart of a man who is initially indifferent to and aloof from her, or openly hostile. The heroine thus actively produces love. Her love causes her to become loved in return, dissolves the indifference of the other and replaces antagonism with devotion.

If the ethos of romantic love is simply understood as the means whereby a woman meets Mr Right, it appears shallow indeed. Yet although in literature, as in life, it is sometimes represented in this way, the capturing of the heart of the other is in fact a process of the creation of a mutual narrative biography. The heroine tames, softens and alters the seemingly intractable masculinity of her love object, making it possible for mutual affection to become the main guiding-line of their lives together.

The intrinsically subversive character of the romantic love complex was for a long while held in check by the association of love with marriage and motherhood; and by the idea that true love, once found, is for ever. When marriage, for many of the population, effectively *was* for ever, the structural congruence between romantic love and sexual partnership was clear-cut. The result may often have been years of unhappiness, given the tenuous connection between love as a formula for marriage and the demands of getting on later. Yet an effective, if not particularly rewarding, marriage could be sustained by a division of labour between the sexes, with the domain of the husband that of paid work and the wife that of the home. We can see in this regard how important the confining of female sexuality to marriage was as a mark of the 'respectable' woman. For this at the same time allowed men to maintain their distance from the burgeoning realm of intimacy and kept the state of being married as a primary aim of women.

NOTES

1 Bronislaw Malinowski: *The Sexual Life of Savages*, London: Routledge, 1929, p. 69.
2 Quoted in Martin S. Bergmann: *The Anatomy of Loving*, New York: Columbia, 1987, p. 4.
3 The term is Stendhal's, but I do not follow his meaning of it, or the classification of types of love that he offered. One might note in parenthesis that, in the early period of its development, social science was closely intertwined with speculation about the nature of love, and also about the divisions between the sexes. Stendhal was strongly influenced by Destutt de Tracy and referred to his work on love as 'a book of ideology'. He meant by this a 'discourse on ideas', but it also takes the form of a social investigation. Comte's fascination with love is documented in his later writings and evidenced by his association with Clothilde de Vaux. By the 'classic' period of the formation of modern sociology, however, these influences had become submerged. Durkheim, for example, who drew extensively on Comte in other respects, had little time for Comte's later work and referred to it with some scorn.
4 Francesco Alberoni: *Falling in Love*, New York: Random House, 1983.
5 Michael Mitterauer and Reinhard Sieder: *The European Family*, Oxford: Blackwell, 1982, pp. 126–9. These claims are controversial among historians, however.
6 This is discussed in a particularly subtle way in Niklas Luhmann: *Love as Passion*, Cambridge: Polity, 1986, ch. 5.
7 Beatrice Gottlieb: 'The meaning of clandestine marriage', in Robert Wheaton and Tamara K. Hareven: *Family and Sexuality in French History*, Philadelphia: University of Pennsylvania Press, 1980.
8 Max Weber: *The Protestant Ethic and the Spirit of Capitalism*, London: Allen and Unwin, 1976.
9 Lawrence Stone: *The Family, Sex and Marriage in England 1500–1800*, Harmondsworth: Pelican, 1982, pp. 189ff.

10 Ibid., p. 189.
11 Ann Dally: *Inventing Motherhood*, London: Burnett, 1982. See also Elizabeth Badinter: *Myth of Motherhood*, London: Souvenir, 1981.
12 Mary Ryan: *The Cradle of the Middle Class*, Cambridge: Cambridge University Press , 1981, p. 102.
13 Francesca M. Cancian: *Love in America*, Cambridge: Cambridge University Press, 1987, p. 21.
14 Quoted in ibid., p. 15.
15 Nancy Cott: *The Bonds of Womanhood*, New Haven: Yale University Press, 1977; Janice Raymond: *A Passion for Friends*, London: Women's Press, 1986.
16 Janice A. Radway: *Reading the Romance*, Chapel Hill: University of North Carolina Press, 1984.

4

LOVE, COMMITMENT AND THE PURE RELATIONSHIP

In the late 1980s, Sharon Thompson carried out an investigation of the attitudes, values and sexual behaviour of 150 American teenagers from different class and ethnic backgrounds.[1] She found major differences between the ways in which the boys discussed sex (they did not often speak of love) in the course of her lengthy interviews with them and the responses of the girls. The boys appeared unable to talk about sex in a narrative form, as a connection to an envisaged future.[2] They spoke mainly about sporadic sexual episodes, such as early heterosexual play or diverse sexual conquests. When she questioned the girls, on the other hand, Thompson found that almost every individual she talked to, with little prompting, could produce lengthy stories 'imbued with the discoveries, anguish, and elation of intimate relations'.[3] The girls, she says, had something approaching the skills of professional novelists in their ability to recount a detailed and complex tale; many talked for several hours with little contribution needed from the interviewer.

The fluent nature of these narratives of self, Thompson argues, derived in large part from the fact that they had been rehearsed. They were the result of the many hours of conversations teenage girls have with one another, during the course of which feelings and hopes are discussed and shaped. Thompson accepts that, as an individual from an older generation, the narratives recounted may have been partly edited for her benefit. But she was also drawn in as a sounding-board for reflexive interpretation on the part of the interviewees. She felt she 'had been entrusted with something as valuable, as telling and prophetic as a first love when the lover reads it, like an omen, for the future'. For, as a further reflexive resonance, she herself admits to an 'addiction to romance'.[4]

The quest-romance

The main thematic device of the girls' stories was what Thompson labels the 'quest-romance'. Romance gears sexuality into an anticipated future in which sexual encounters are seen as detours on the way to an eventual love relationship. Sex is, as it were, a sparking device, with romance as the quest for destiny. The search for romantic love here, however, no longer means deferring sexual activity until the desired relationship comes along. Having sex with a new partner may be the start of the fateful encounter which is sought after, but more than likely it is not.

The following is a description given by an interviewee of a romance:

> We discovered that we lived sort of in the same neighbourhood, and we started taking the bus home together. Then we discovered we didn't want to take the bus home together. We wanted to walk because it meant more time talking. Both of us had our own ideas about the world . . . We'd start talking about school, and we'd end up talking about the situation in China . . . and within three months, I was so in love . . . it was amazing.[5]

Amazing, yes – or it would have been to a researcher on teenage sexuality twenty-five years earlier – because the romance in question was a lesbian one. One of the findings that comes through strongly in Thompson's work is that sexual diversity exists alongside the persistence of notions of romance, although sometimes in an uneasy and conflictual relation. The lesbian girls among Thompson's interviewees appeared to find romance as compelling as did the heterosexuals.

'Loss of virginity' for a boy, as from time immemorial, continues today to be a misnomer: for boys, first sexual experience is a plus, a gain. It is a talisman which points to the future; not, however, in respect of core aspects of the self, but as one among other emblems of male capability. For girls, virginity is still something seen as given up. The question is not, for most, whether or not to do so as part of early sexual experience, but how to choose the right time and circumstance. The event connects directly to romantic narratives. Boys expect to force the issue of sexual initiation, girls to 'slow things down'. The query girls pose to themselves, as well as implicitly to their first partner, whoever he (or she) may be, is: will my sexuality allow me to determine the path of my future life? Will it give me sexual power? First sexual experience is for many a test of whether or not a future romantic scenario can be achieved.

As the term suggests, the quest-romance is not for these girls a passive set of aspirations – 'some day my prince will come'. Painful and anxiety-ridden in many respects, it is nevertheless an active process of engagement with future time. Echoing Rubin, Thompson found that the girls she spoke to did not have to fight to achieve sexual freedom: such freedom exists, and the problem is to make something of it in the face of male attitudes which still carry more than an echo of the past. The girls therefore emerge as the main social experimenters here. Thompson expresses this very well:

> To an extent, teenage girls are struggling with the problem nineteenth-century feminists predicted when they argued against breaking the connection between sex and reproduction on the grounds that it constituted the only way women had to persuade men to commit themselves to a relationship. But it is, finally, not a problem of enforcement, but of vision. It demands facing the deconstruction of sex, romance and intimacy and renegotiating the bargain between the genders.[6]

Under the strain of these tasks, some girls try to retreat to pre-existing ideas and modes of behaviour – acceptance of the double standard, 'flypaper dreams of motherhood', hopes for eternal love. Most find themselves breaking away from earlier-established norms and taboos, adapting them in ways in which a great deal of emotional energy is invested, but which are quite provisional and open to restructuring in the light of possible future events.

By their late teens, many of the girls have already had experience of unhappy love affairs, and are well aware that romance can no longer be equated with permanence. In a highly reflexive society they come into contact with, and in their television watching and reading actively search out, numerous discussions about sex, relationships and influences affecting the position of women. The fragmentary elements of the romantic love complex with which these girls are grappling in seeking to take practical control of their lives are no longer linked wholly to marriage. Virtually all recognise that they will be in paid work for much of their lives, and most see the importance of work skills as a basis for their future autonomy. Only a few of the girls among Thompson's interviewees, however – mostly those from middle-class backgrounds – regard work as a major source of meaning for their future. Thus one girl said, 'My idea of what I want to do right now is to get a career that I love . . . if I marry somebody or even live with somebody and they leave me, I won't have anything to worry about because I'll be totally independent.' Yet, as Thompson found with others, she quickly reverted to matters of romance and sexuality: 'I want the ideal relationship with a guy. I guess I want someone to love me and care about me as much as I do them.'[7]

Women, marriage, relationships

It is only over the past generation that striking out on one's own, for women, has meant leaving the parental home. In previous periods, for all but a small proportion of women, leaving home meant getting married. In contrast to most men, the majority of women continue to identify entering the outside world with forming attachments. As many commentators have noted, even when an individual is still single and only anticipating future relationships, men normally speak in terms of 'I', whereas female narratives of self tend to be couched in terms of 'we'. The 'individualised speech' apparent in the above quotation is qualified by a surreptitious 'we' – someone who will 'love and care' and make a 'we' from the 'me'.

In contrast to those in younger age-groups today, the experience of older women was almost always framed in terms of marriage, even if the person in question did not marry. Emily Hancock investigated the life-histories of twenty American women, from various class origins, aged between thirty and seventy-five in the late 1980s. Some were still in their first marriages, others had remarried, were divorced or widowed. Marriage was to them the core experience of a woman's life – although many have had retrospectively to reconstruct their past, because when they first got married, marriage was very different from what it is now.

Let us follow for a little while the history of Wendy, who

was thirty-nine when Hancock interviewed her. Wendy's life-story demonstrates an increasing reflexive awareness of self, brought about partly by outside social changes, and partly by personal crises and transitions that she has had to surmount. Wendy is the oldest of four children from an affluent New England family in which the parents followed fairly strict codes of 'proper behaviour'. She broke away from her parents' control by means of marriage, and did so actively and consciously, through an elopement (a term which, during a period of a few decades, has become archaic). Wendy saw marriage as equivalent to entry into adulthood. She thought of it as 'a re-creation of a cocoon at the same time that you're also a fully grown butterfly'.

Her attachment to her prospective husband facilitated her independence, at least as she saw things then: 'This relationship with a new person was the first really independent action I took. So many other things followed from that one.' Yet her act of autonomy was also one presuming material dependence. 'I suppose it would have been more radical not to have married at all. That would have been the most radical thing, but that was never an option for me. I never thought of myself as a person who would not be married. It was a given.' She didn't want only to be a housewife, and was determined not to have as parochial a life as her mother, whose prime concern had always been the home. Wendy became a schoolteacher and found the career satisfying. She did not give up the job when she became pregnant, but moved to half-time teaching.

Then her husband was killed in a freak accident. She underwent a severe crisis, and lost her grip on her sense of her adult self. It was not just the bereavement, but the loss of the attachment upon which she had based her feelings of security and accomplishment which were traumatic. She felt 'thrust back into adolescence', even though she had a child to look after. Her parents expected her to go back and live with them; she successfully resisted after having come to realise how much she had depended upon the marriage for a sense of integrity. Her second marriage, like her first, was entered into for love, and was 'part of putting myself back together'. But by this point she 'had more perspective' than when she married for the first time: 'It is doing these things with a self-consciousness that comes after scrambling that helps you realise potential. You shape it in a clearer way, like a sculpture.' Wendy had further children by her second marriage; she was content with her life, still found satisfaction in her paid work, but was not ambitious for further career achievement.

Compare Wendy's experience with that of Helen, aged forty-nine when contacted by the researcher. When she was growing up Helen had, in her own words, 'lacked self-confidence to a pathological degree'. At college, she met and married a professor who was rapidly making a reputation for himself in his chosen field. Having abandoned her education in order to get married, her sense of self-worth became largely dependent upon her involvement with the aspirations and achievements of her husband. She occupied part of his life, as she later put it, as 'a tenant' or 'a janitor'. She and her husband were living in university housing when he announced he wanted a divorce; since he was the one with the faculty position, she had to leave, taking their child to live with her. Unlike Wendy, her parents did not invite her to come back home or offer much moral or material support.

Overwhelmed at first by desperation and beset by loneliness, Helen eventually managed to go back to college part-time and finish her degree. None the less, she found herself for some while stuck in low-grade 'women's jobs' until she managed to get a post in publishing, and had at the time of the research become a successful editor. She is described by Hancock as a person with a sharp, sarcastic manner, given to sardonic wit. Yet her surface competence disguised attitudes of despair and self-hate with which the ending of her marriage had left her and from which she had never recovered. She felt caught up in a life that was 'empty and arid'. Rather than seeking to shape her future, she was continuing 'to drift toward infinity'. She concluded: 'You ask me what my adult life has been? A vacuum, that's what it's been. By the age of thirty-five, I was a corpse. And now I am almost fifty and I can't even account for the intervening fifteen years. I've brought up my child, but my sense of time has disappeared.'[8]

A reasonably contented and fulfilled woman, a lonely, embittered one: banal enough stories, each of them, although in both cases infused with considerable pain. What do they tell us about love, since love is not a dominating theme in the narratives of either individual? It would be easy to say, and impossible to dispute, that marriage was a trap for both women, even if a trap into which each deliberately plunged. Wendy was able to recover from the loss of her husband, whereas Helen could not do so, and became bowed down by the oppressive force of circumstances which women alone so often face. Each married for love – Wendy twice – but each, without fully realising it, married as an assertion of independence and as a means of forging a definite self-identity. Who knows whether Wendy would still be able to take effective charge of her life if her second husband left her?

Like most of the women interviewed by Hancock, both sought to get away from the lives their mothers lived, which they identified with constrained domesticity. The process was tensionful, because each sought to distance herself from her mother without rejecting femininity. We do not see here the perpetuating of attitudes linking love and marriage as a 'final state'; but nor is there an attempt simply to enter a male world through the adoption of instrumental values. These women, as with the others portrayed in Hancock's book, are in a real sense pioneers moving through unmapped territory, who chart out shifts in self-identity as they confront and are confronted by changes in the nature of marriage, the family and work.

The paradox is that marriage is used as a means of achieving a measure of autonomy. Romantic love, I suggested earlier, is a gamble against the future, an orientation to the control of future time on the part of women who became specialists in matters of (what now has come to be understood as) intimacy. There was an almost inevitable connection between love and marriage, for many women, in the earlier periods of modern development. But even then, quite apart from the interventions of foresightful feminist authors, women were *de facto* exploring other paths. The severance between marriage and its traditional roots in 'external' factors imposed itself much more forcefully upon women than men, who could find in marriage and the family primarily a refuge from economic individualism. For men, colonising the future in terms of an anticipated economic career tended to push out of the reckoning the parallel, but substantively very different, form of colonising time offered by romantic love. For them, on the surface, at least, love remained closer to *amour passion*.

Marriage for Wendy and Helen, when they first entered it, was already contradictory, but also on the point of becoming infused with a higher level of reflexivity. It had not yet been prised free of its 'external' anchors, and provided a distinct status for women as wives and mothers. Yet, even in the early part of their lives, it was already not just for them a question of 'finding a man', but linked to tasks and concerns quite different from those of their mothers' generation. Women like Wendy and Helen helped prepare the way for a restructuring of intimate life behind which stands the whole weight of the changes discussed in Chapter 1. If the teenage girls do not speak much about marriage, it is not because they have successfully made a transition to a non-domestic future, but because they are participants in, and contributors to, a major reorganisation in what marriage, and other forms of close personal tie, actually are. They talk of relationships rather than marriage as such, and they are right to do so.

The term 'relationship', meaning a close and continuing emotional tie to another, has only come into general usage relatively recently. To be clear what is at stake here, we can introduce the term *pure relationship* to refer to this phenomenon.[9] A pure relationship has nothing to do with sexual purity, and is a limiting concept rather than only a descriptive one. It refers to a situation where a social relation is entered into for its own sake, for what can be derived by each person from a sustained association with another; and which is continued only in so far as it is thought by both parties to deliver enough satisfactions for each individual to stay within it. Love used to be tied to sexuality, for most of the sexually 'normal' population, through marriage; but now the two are connected more and more via the pure relationship. Marriage – for many, but by no means all groups in the population – has veered increasingly towards the form of a pure relationship, with many ensuing consequences. The pure relationship, to repeat, is part of a generic restructuring of intimacy. It emerges in other contexts of sexuality besides heterosexual marriage; it is in some causally related ways parallel to the development of plastic sexuality. The romantic love complex helped carve open a way to the formation of pure relationships in the domain of sexuality, but has now become weakened by some of the very influences it helped create.

Women, men, romantic love

All this so far has been mostly about women. If the romantic love complex has been developed, and also later in some part dissolved, primarily by women, what has happened to men? Have men remained untouched by the changes which women have helped bring about, save in their role as reactionary defenders of entrenched privilege? That men are participants in the everyday experiments described in this book goes almost without saying. But I feel justified in offering an interpretation of the transmutation of romantic love which largely excludes men. Men are the laggards in the transitions now occurring – and in a certain sense have been so ever since the late eighteenth century. In Western culture at least, today is the first period in which men are finding themselves *to be* men, that is, as possessing a problematic 'masculinity'. In previous times, men have assumed that their activities constituted 'history', whereas women existed almost out of time, doing the same as they had always done.

Men, like women, fall in love and have done so throughout the recorded past. They have also over the last two centuries been influenced by the development of ideals of romantic love, but in a different way from women. Those men who have come too much under the sway of such notions of love have been set apart from the majority as 'romantics', in a particular sense of that term. They are, as it were, foppish dreamers, who have succumbed to female power. Such men have given up the division between unsullied and impure women so central to male sexuality. The romantic does not, nevertheless, treat women as equals. He is in thrall to a particular woman (or to several women in sequence) and he would build his life around her; but his succumbing is not a gesture of equality. He is not really a participant in the emerging exploration of intimacy, but more of a throwback to previous times. The romantic in this instance is not someone who has intuitively understood the nature of love as a mode of organising personal life in relation to the colonising of future time and to the construction of self-identity.

For most men, romantic love stands in tension with the

imperatives of seduction. This observation means more than just that the rhetoric of romantic love is stock in trade for most Lotharios. Since the beginnings of the transformations affecting marriage and personal life, men by and large have excluded themselves from the developing domain of the intimate. The connections between romantic love and intimacy were suppressed, and falling in love remained closely bound up with access: access to women whose virtue or reputation was protected until, at least, a union was sanctified by marriage. Men have tended to be 'specialists in love' only in respect of the techniques of seduction or conquest.

There has always been a gulf between the sexes in terms of experience, upbringing and education. 'Those impossible women! How they do get around us! The poet was right: can't live with them or without them' (Aristophanes). In the nineteenth century, however, for reasons already discussed, women became opaque to men in a new way. They were rendered mysterious, as Foucault maintains, by the very discourses that sought to know them, which made female sexuality a 'problem' and treated their diseases as forms of social disqualification coming from murky depths. But they also became puzzling by virtue of the very changes they were helping to introduce.

What do men want? In one sense the answer has been clear and understood by both sexes from the nineteenth century onwards. Men want status among other men, conferred by material rewards and conjoined to rituals of male solidarity. But the male sex here misread a key trend in the trajectory of development of modernity. For men self-identity was sought after in work, and they failed – we always have to add, by and large – to understand that the reflexive project of self involves an emotional reconstruction of the past in order to project a coherent narrative towards the future. Their unconscious emotional reliance upon women was the mystery whose answer they sought in women themselves; and the quest for self-identity became concealed within this unacknowledged dependence. What men wanted was something which women had in some part already achieved; it is no wonder that male authors, including the narrator of *My Secret Life*, became obsessed with the secret that only women could reveal, but which the piling up of amorous conquests wholly failed to disclose.

Romantic versus confluent love

In the current era, ideals of romantic love tend to fragment under the pressure of female sexual emancipation and autonomy. The clash between the romantic love complex and the pure relationship takes various forms, each of which tends to become more and more displayed to general view as a result of increasing institutional reflexivity. Romantic love depends upon projective identification, the projective identification of *amour passion*, as the means whereby prospective partners become attracted and then bound to one another. Projection here creates a feeling of wholeness with the other, no doubt strengthened by established differences between masculinity and femininity, each defined in terms of an antithesis. The traits of the other are 'known' in a sort of intuitive sense. Yet in other respects projective identification cuts across the development of a relationship whose continuation depends upon intimacy. Opening oneself out to the other, the condition of what I shall call *confluent love*, is in some ways the opposite of projective identification, even if such identification sometimes sets up a pathway to it.

Confluent love is active, contingent love, and therefore jars with the 'for-ever', 'one-and-only' qualities of the romantic love complex. The 'separating and divorcing society' of today here appears as an effect of the emergence of confluent love rather than its cause. The more confluent love becomes consolidated as a real possibility, the more the finding of a 'special person' recedes and the more it is the 'special relationship' that counts.

In contrast to confluent love, romantic love has always been imbalanced in gender terms, as a result of influences already discussed. Romantic love has long had an egalitarian strain, intrinsic to the idea that a relationship can derive from the emotional involvement of two people, rather than from external social criteria. *De facto*, however, romantic love is thoroughly skewed in terms of power. For women dreams of romantic love have all too often led to grim domestic subjection. Confluent love presumes equality in emotional give and take, the more so the more any particular love tie approximates closely to the prototype of the pure relationship. Love here only develops to the degree to which intimacy does, to the degree to which each partner is prepared to reveal concerns and needs to the other and to be vulnerable to that other. The masked emotional dependence of men has inhibited their willingness, and their capacity, to be made thus vulnerable. The ethos of romantic love has in some part sustained this orientation, in the sense in which the desirable man has often been represented as cold and unapproachable. Yet since such love dissolves these characteristics, which are revealed as a front, recognition of male emotional vulnerability is evidently present.

Romantic love is sexual love, but it brackets off the *ars erotica*. Sexual satisfaction and happiness, especially in the fantasy form of romance, are supposedly guaranteed by the very erotic force which romantic love provokes. Confluent love for the first time introduces the *ars erotica* into the core of the conjugal relationship and makes the achievement of reciprocal sexual pleasure a key element in whether the relationship is sustained or dissolved. The cultivation of sexual skills, the capability of giving and experiencing sexual satisfaction, on the part of both sexes, become organised reflexively via a multitude of sources of sexual information, advice and training.

In non-Western cultures, as mentioned earlier, the *ars erotica* was usually a female speciality, and almost always limited to specific groups; erotic arts were cultivated by concubines, prostitutes or the members of minority religious communities. Confluent love develops as an ideal in a society where almost everyone has the chance to become sexually accomplished; and it presumes the disappearance of the schism between 'respectable' women and those who in some way lie outside the pale of orthodox social life. Unlike romantic love, confluent love is not necessarily monogamous, in the sense of sexual exclusiveness. What holds the pure relationship together is the acceptance on the part of each partner, 'until further notice', that each gains sufficient benefit from the relation to make its continuance worthwhile. Sexual exclusiveness here has a role in the relationship to the degree to which the partners mutually deem it desirable or essential.

One further very important contrast between romantic and confluent love should be noted: like the pure relationship in general, confluent love has no specific connection to heterosexuality. Ideas of romance have been extended to homosexual love, and have some purchase upon femininity/masculinity distinctions developed among same-sex partners. I have already pointed out that romantic love contains features which tend to override sexual difference. None the less, the romantic love complex plainly has been oriented mainly towards the heterosexual couple. Confluent love, while not necessarily androgynous, and still perhaps structured around difference, presumes a model of the pure relationship in which knowing the traits of the other is central. It is a version of love in which a person's sexuality is one factor that has to be negotiated as part of a relationship.

I want to leave aside for the time being how far confluent

love in practice forms part of sexual relationships today. For there are other aspects and implications of the pure relationship, and its association with self-identity and personal autonomy, which have first of all to be discussed. In such discussion, I shall quite often – although in critical vein – take therapeutic works and self-help manuals as my guide. Not because they offer accurate accounts of the changes affecting personal life: most in any case are essentially practical handbooks. Rather, they are expressions of processes of reflexivity which they chart out and help shape. Many are also emancipatory: they point towards changes that might release individuals from influences which block their autonomous development. They are texts of our time in a comparable sense to the medieval manuals of manners analysed by Norbert Elias, or the works of etiquette utilised by Erving Goffman in his studies of the interaction order.

NOTES

1 Sharon Thompson: 'Search for tomorrow: or feminism and the reconstruction of teen romance', in Carole S. Vance: *Pleasure and Danger. Exploring Female Sexuality*, London: Pandora, 1989.
2 Ibid., p. 350.
3 Ibid., p. 351.
4 Ibid., p. 351.
5 Quoted in ibid., p. 361.
6 Ibid., p. 360.
7 Ibid., p. 356.
8 All quotations are from Emily Hancock: *The Girl Within*, London: Pandora, 1990.
9 Anthony Giddens: *Modernity and Self-Identity*, Cambridge: Polity, 1991.

5

LOVE, SEX AND OTHER ADDICTIONS

'I looked down the front of a woman's dress when we were making sandwiches for the hungry at the church mission . . . I tried to pick up another patient in line at the VD clinic . . . I slept with my boyfriend's best friend when he was out of town . . .' Indiscretions revealed in the privacy of the Catholic confessional? No, these are public statements made at a meeting of Sex Addicts Anonymous.[1] SAA derived from the treatment of alcoholism, and is directly modelled upon Alcoholics Anonymous.[2] SAA groups adopt the 'twelve-step' recovery method favoured by Alcoholics Anonymous, according to which individuals agree first of all to accept that they are in the grip of a compulsion they are powerless to control. The first step in the 'Big Book' of Alcoholics Anonymous reads: 'We admitted we were powerless over alcohol – that our lives had become unmanageable.' SAA members are required to start with the same admission and thence progress towards overcoming their subjection to their sexual needs.

In an interesting – and significant – reversal of the trends remarked upon by Foucault, the proponents of SAA, who are mostly not medical personnel, have sought to medicalise sex addiction. The 'condition', they propose, should be listed in diagnostic handbooks as 'hyperactive sexual desire disorder'. The notion may seem far-fetched, all the more so as it is claimed that a very substantial proportion of the population is afflicted by it. Yet much the same is true of alcohol addiction, which according to some estimates affects as many as one-quarter of all adults in the United States. It took a long while for alcoholism to be accepted officially in medical circles as an addiction, even though it has a definite physiological basis.

Sex addiction might at first sight look like just another eccentricity – or perhaps a new mode of exploiting a gullible populace, since a recognised psychiatric category can help interested parties qualify for medical funding, generate research support and present themselves as a new breed of experts. But there is more going on here than such a view would suggest, both in the area of sexual activity specifically and on a broader level. Sex is only one of a proliferation of addictions recognised over the past few years. It is possible to become addicted, among other things, to drugs, food, work, smoking, shopping, exercise, gambling – and, apart from the specifically sexual component, love and relationships also.[3] Why should addiction have come to be so widely spoken of over the relatively recent period? To answer this question, which has a bearing upon my arguments in the whole of the book, let us look at the issue of sex addiction and consider in what sense, if any, it is a real phenomenon rather than a superficial therapeutic novelty.

Sex and desire

'Women want love, men want sex.' If this crude stereotype were true, there could be no question of sex addiction. Men's appetite for sex, with as many partners as possible, would simply be a defining characteristic of their masculinity. Women's desire for love would override any proclivity towards sex, which would be the price for acquiring the rewards of loving and being loved.

Yet this hoary old observation, at least in the present-day world, could be turned around. Women want sex? Yes, for the first time women collectively, rather than as specialists in an *ars erotica*, are able to seek out sexual pleasure as a basic component of their lives and their relationships. Men want love? Certainly they do, despite appearances to the contrary – perhaps more than the majority of women, although in ways that still remain to be looked into. For men's position in the public domain has been achieved at the expense of their exclusion from the transformation of intimacy.

So let us see where we get to if the saying is reversed. I shall begin by following the fortunes of Gerri, a young woman who contacted an SAA group in the Minneapolis area, and who became a participant in a research project into female sex addiction reported by Charlotte Kasl.[4] Before she joined SAA – and, in fits and starts afterwards – Gerri led a life as schizophrenic as any man who might have mixed probity in work activities with the calculated pursuit of sexual conquests in the non-work part of his life. During the day she was a teaching assistant in a school. In the evenings she sometimes attended other classes, but also frequented singles bars and in the months before becoming affiliated to SAA she was sexually involved simultaneously with four different men, each of whom was ignorant of the existence of the others. She reached a crisis in her life when she found that, in spite of taking greater precautions than before, she had contracted venereal disease (for the twelfth time in her life). In order to trace back others who might have been infected, she would have had to contact no fewer than fourteen men with whom she was sexually involved over a short period.

She was unable to bring herself to do so, partly because she could not face up to the indignity of making the necessary telephone calls, partly because she was worried that the men she had been seeing regularly would discover her duplicity towards them. Gerri first found out about the notion of sex addiction when she came across an article on the subject in the local paper, mentioning a sex dependence clinic at the hospital. The thought of going to the clinic crossed her mind, but instead she called up one of her men friends and spent the night having sex with him. She contacted the clinic only several days later, after a further sexual episode. Gerri and her sister went to a bar and picked up two men. Driving back to her apartment with one of them, she was involved in a car accident. She reported:

> I was in a state of shock when we got home. Even so, I wanted to be sexual. Usually with sex I can make everything go away, but I couldn't that night. During sex I felt dead and sick to my stomach. I was relieved when the guy went home during the night. I had no interest in seeing him again, but my ego was outraged that he didn't call me the next day. I pride myself on getting men to chase after me.[5]

Gerri felt her life to be out of control and frequently contemplated suicide. She tried to steer clear of sexual encounters for several months after joining the SAA group, to which the clinic had referred her. During this time she was arrested for welfare fraud: the authorities claimed that, prior to getting her teaching job, she had obtained welfare benefits to which she was not entitled. The charge was a dubious one, and she became something of a local *cause célèbre*, receiving the support of several women's rights organisations.

In court, several other women charged with similar offences appeared on the stand before her, all of whom pleaded guilty; she, however, stated that she was not guilty and eventually the charge against her was dropped. Gerri subsequently became a prominent member of a group which contested cases in which women claiming welfare were penalised. She spoke of coming to see 'how women are demeaned and what harsh sentences they receive for trying to survive'. Fighting for their rights, she 'could feel my own purpose in life unfolding'. Previously, she said, 'sex was a way to get power . . . the only way I knew'.[6] She began a new relationship with a man, moved in with him and struggled not to become sexually involved with anyone else.

Was Gerri acting in the same way as a long line of male seducers, trying to sample as varied a sex life as she could manage to achieve? The answer, I think, is a qualified yes. She was engaged in some sort of quest, through the use of sexuality, which can only be described as a frustrated search for self-identity; this endeavour was not the conventional quest-romance. She actively pursued men and did not just wait at home for them to call her. Her self-esteem was bound up with her sexual prowess, including her ability to gain as well as give sexual pleasure; and she kept a tally of the men she had 'conquered'.

Yet there is a desperate, tragic undertone to her story, which also sometimes comes through in male experiences of a parallel kind, but is normally less evident there. There may very well be some women today who, without too many psychic problems, adopt something close to the traditional male attitude towards sexuality as an organising dynamic of their own sexual conduct. But if there are such women, Gerri was certainly not one of them, for her behaviour involved her in great suffering. It turns out that both of her parents were alcoholics, and her father combined his alcoholism with a tendency to violent rages, which were quite often directed against his children. He sexually abused all four daughters in the family; Gerri learned to be 'nice' to him – in other words to accept his sexual advances – so as to protect herself and her sisters from likely beatings. On one occasion she reported her father to the local child care officer. When a social worker visited the family her father was able to persuade him that nothing was wrong; but her father later took out his wrath on her and she did not dare make any further public complaints.

Gerri 'wanted sex': she was trying to integrate an openness to new sexual experiences with the other exigencies of her life. She learned early on that sex gave her a measure of control in a world over which her real influence was limited and problematic. Gerri felt her life to be quite inauthentic, and it was indeed so: she was effectively behaving like a sexually adventurous man without the material support, or generalised normative acceptance, which most such men can take for granted. She could call men, and actively seek out new sexual partners, but could not readily pursue a sexual contact beyond a certain point in the way in which a man might do. Many, perhaps most, men still find it inappropriate, and threatening, for women to behave towards them as they routinely do in reverse. The need for constant sexual approval had become part of Gerri's character – but she had to search for such endorsement in social settings which men control.

The nature of addiction

Before deciding whether or not it is reasonable to speak of Gerri's behaviour as sex addiction, let me move back to a more general plane and consider what the idea of addiction might mean. The notion of addiction was originally linked almost wholly to chemical dependency, upon alcohol or drugs of various sorts. Once the idea had been medicalised, it was defined as a physical pathology: addiction in this sense refers to a state of the organism. Such a concept, however, conceals the fact that addiction is expressed in compulsive behaviour. Even in the case of chemical dependency, addiction is measured *de facto* in terms of the consequences of the habit for an individual's control over her or his life, plus the difficulties of giving up that habit.

All social life is substantially routinised: we have regular modes of activity which we repeat from day to day, and which give form to our individual lives as well as reproducing larger institutions to which our conduct contributes. But such routines are not all of a piece. Craig Nakken makes a useful set of distinctions between patterns of action, habits, compulsions and addictions.[7] A pattern is simply a routine which helps order daily life, but which an individual can alter when needs be. Thus someone may take the dog for a walk most mornings, but can switch to evenings if necessary. A habit is a more psychologically binding form of repetitive behaviour than a pattern; a distinct effort of the will is needed to alter or break it. Habitual activities are often described by the word 'always' – 'I always eat dinner at eight o'clock in the evening.'

A compulsion is a form of behaviour which an individual finds very difficult, or impossible, to stop through willpower alone, the enactment of which produces a release of tension. Compulsions usually take the form of stereotyped personal rituals, such as where an individual has to wash forty or fifty times a day in order to feel clean. Compulsive behaviour is associated with a feeling of loss of control over self; someone may carry out the ritual actions in a sort of trance-like state. Failure to engage in them causes an upsurge of anxiety.

Addictions are compulsive, but are not minor rituals; they colour large areas of an individual's life. An addiction includes each of the aspects of behaviour just mentioned and more besides. It can be defined as a patterned habit that is compulsively engaged in, withdrawal from which generates an unmanageable anxiety. Addictions provide a source of comfort for the individual, by assuaging anxiety, but this experience is always more or less transient.[8] All addictions are essentially narcotising, but the chemical effect, if there is one, is not an essential element of the addictive experience.

Some of the specific characteristics of addictions are the following:

1. The 'high'. The high is what individuals seek out when they look for, in Erving Goffman's terms, where the action is[9] – an experience which is set apart from the ordinary, from the mundane characteristics of everyday life. It is a momentary feeling of elation which the person enjoys when a 'special' sensation is produced – a moment of release. The high is sometimes, although not always, a feeling of triumph as well as relaxation. Prior to a process of addiction a high is an intrinsically rewarding experience. Once an addictive pattern is established, however, the element of release predominates over the inherent characteristics of whatever sensations are involved.

2. The 'fix'. When a person is addicted to a specific experience or form of behaviour, the endeavour to achieve a high becomes translated into the need for a fix. The fix eases anxiety and introduces the individual into the narcotising phase of the addiction. The fix is psychologically necessary, but sooner or later is succeeded by depression and feelings of emptiness; and the cycle begins again.

3. The high and the fix are both forms of 'time out'. The usual strivings of the individual are temporarily in stasis and appear remote; the person, as it were, is in 'another world' and may regard his or her ordinary activities with cynical amusement or even disdain. Yet these feelings are often subject to abrupt reversal, and might turn to disgust with the addictive pattern. Such disaffection usually takes the form of despair that the addiction cannot be controlled; it is something that happens despite the individual's 'best intentions'.

4. The addictive experience is a giving up of self, a temporary abandonment of that reflexive concern with the

protection of self-identity generic to most circumstances of day-to-day life. Some forms of high – those associated with religious ecstasy, for example – specifically relate the experience to the overcoming or loss of self. In addictions, however, such sensations are normally a secular part of the behaviour pattern; the feeling of displacement of self is intrinsic to the sensation of release from anxiety.

5. The sense of loss of self is later succeeded by feelings of shame and remorse. Addictions are not ordinarily steady-state forms of behaviour, but tend to escalate in their importance. A negative feedback process can occur in which a growing dependence upon the addictive behaviour generates, not increasing feelings of well-being, but panic and self-destructiveness.

6. The addictive experience feels like a very 'special' one and it is so in the sense that at the time nothing else will do. Yet addictions are often functionally equivalent, in terms of the psychic condition of the individual. A person will struggle free of one addiction, only to succumb to another, and become locked into a new compulsive behaviour pattern. She or he might couple two forms of addictive behaviour, such as drinking and heavy smoking, or sometimes use one temporarily to stave off the cravings created by the other. Addictive behaviour may be 'layered' in the individual's psychological makeup, such that more minor addictive traits, or compulsions, cover over the core addiction. The fact that addictions tend to be functionally interchangeable lends strong support to the conclusion that they signal an underlying incapacity to cope with certain sorts of anxiety.

7. The loss of self and the self-disgust characteristic of addictions are not necessarily to be identified with indulgence. All addictions are pathologies of self-discipline, but such deviations may go in two directions – towards letting go, or towards tightening up. We can see each of these tendencies expressed in food addictions, which can take the

form of compulsive over-eating and/or anorexic fasting. Although bulimia and anorexia appear opposed, they are two sides of one coin and frequently co-exist as propensities of the same individual.

Addiction, reflexivity, self-autonomy

In Western countries, people from varying strata have long consumed alcohol as well as other drugs. But they were not called addicts. Until the nineteenth century, the regular drinking of alcohol, for example, was only seen as a 'social problem' to the degree to which it led to public disorder. The idea that one can be an addict dates from the mid-nineteenth century or so; the term did not come into general use until later, and precedes by some while the widespread application of the term alcoholic addiction. The invention of the addict, in Foucault's terms, is a control mechanism, a new network of 'power/knowledge'. Yet it also marks one step along the road towards the emergence of the reflexive project of self, which is both emancipatory and constraining. The addict, after all, is someone who is 'intemperate', a word that does not relate only to public order but to a refusal, a disinclination quietly to accept one's lot.

Addiction signals a particular mode of control over parts of one's day-to-day life – and also over the self. The specific importance of addiction can be understood in the following way. Addiction has to be understood in terms of a society in which tradition has more thoroughly been swept away than ever before and in which the reflexive project of self correspondingly assumes an especial importance. Where large areas of a person's life are no longer set by pre-existing patterns and habits, the individual is continually obliged to negotiate life-style options. Moreover – and this is crucial – such choices are not just 'external' or marginal aspects of the individual's attitudes, but define who the individual 'is'. In other words, life-style choices are constitutive of the reflexive narrative of self.[10]

The fact that alcoholism was identified as a physical pathology for some while directed attention away from the connections between addiction, life-style choice and self-identity. The emancipatory promise it held was blocked to the degree to which it was perceived as an illness like any other. Yet the early programme of Alcoholics Anonymous already acknowledged that recovery from addiction meant undertaking profound changes in life-style and a re-examination of self-identity. As with psychotherapy and counselling, those who attend meetings find an atmosphere in which criticism or judgement are suspended. Members are encouraged to reveal their most private concerns and worries in an open way without fear of embarrassment or an abusive response. The leitmotif of these groups is a rewriting of the narrative of self.

In a post-traditional order, the narrative of self has in fact continually to be reworked, and life-style practices brought in line with it, if the individual is to combine personal autonomy with a sense of ontological security. Processes of self-actualisation, however, are very often partial and confined. Hence it is not surprising that addictions are potentially so wide-ranging in nature. Once institutional reflexivity reaches into virtually all parts of everyday social life, almost any pattern or habit can become an addiction. The idea of addiction makes little sense in a traditional culture, where it is normal to do today what one did yesterday. When there was continuity of tradition, and a particular social pattern followed what was long established, as well as sanctioned as right and proper, it could hardly be described as an addiction; nor did it make a statement about specific characteristics of self. Individuals could not pick and choose, but at the same time had no obligation to discover themselves in their actions and habits.

Addictions, then, are a negative index of the degree to which the reflexive project of self moves to centre-stage in late modernity. They are modes of behaviour which intrude, perhaps in a very consequential way, into that project, but refuse to be harnessed to it. In this sense all are harmful to the individual and it is easy to see why the problem of overcoming them now brooks so large in the therapeutic literature. An addiction is an inability to colonise the future and as such transgresses one of the prime concerns with which individuals now reflexively have to cope.

Every addiction is a defensive reaction, and an escape, a recognition of lack of autonomy that casts a shadow over the competence of the self.[11] In the case of minor compulsions, feelings of shame may be limited to mild self-disparagement, an ironic admission that 'I just seem to be hooked on this stuff'. In more pronounced forms of compulsive behaviour the integrity of the self as a whole is menaced. Wider social norms quite profoundly influence whether or not this becomes so. Addictions that are focused in socially acceptable ways are less easily recognised as such, either by the individuals concerned or by others – until, perhaps, certain crisis circumstances intervene. This is often true, as I shall indicate in a minute, of sex and it is true of work. A workaholic in a prestigeful job might go for many years without fully acknowledging the compulsive character of his (or, less commonly, her) activity. Only when other events intervene does the defensive nature of his dedication become apparent – if, for instance, he suffers a breakdown on losing his position or if his marriage collapses. Work, so to speak, has been everything to him, but it has also been a time out, a long-term narcotic experience that dulls other needs or aspirations which he cannot directly manage. He has been accustomed, as the phrase has it, regularly to lose himself in his work.

Implications for sexuality

At this point we can return to the question of sex addiction. Some might be inclined to dispute whether sex could become compulsive in the same sense as work. For the need for regular sexual activity, someone might object, is a basic drive which all adults have; almost everyone is thus addicted to sex in any case. But the existence of a need does not govern the means of its satiation. The need for food is also an elemental drive, yet food addictions have become very prominent today. Sex is compulsive, just like other behaviour patterns, when a person's sexual behaviour is governed by a constant search for a fix which, however, persistently leads to feelings of shame and inadequacy. Addiction is behaviour counterposed to choice, in respect of the reflexive project of self; this observation is just as valid in the case of sex addiction as other forms of behaviour.

Compulsive sexuality has to be understood against the backdrop of circumstances in which sexual experience has become more freely available than ever before, and where sexual identity forms a core part of the narrative of self. Women want sex? Of course they do, if this is understood as staking a claim to sexual autonomy and fulfilment. Yet consider the enormity of the changes which this circumstance presumes. Anyone who believes that the 'repressive hypothesis' contains no truth should ponder the fact that, only some seventy-five years ago, in Britain, unmarried girls who became pregnant were sent in their thousands to reformatories and mental hospitals. The Mental Deficiency Act, passed in 1913, allowed local authorities to certify, and detain indefinitely, unmarried pregnant women who were poor, homeless or just 'immoral'. Since the idea was widely held that illegitimate pregnancy was itself a sign of mental subnormality, the terms of the Act could be, and were, applied very widely indeed. Unmarried women from more

affluent backgrounds who became pregnant could sometimes get illegal abortions – as could poorer women, but at
considerable risk to life – yet otherwise they were effectively
pariahs. Ignorance about sex and reproduction was taken to
imply subnormality, but was widespread. One woman,
born in 1918 in London, interviewed in an oral history study
by Joy Melville, recalls that her mother whispered to her
every night as she went to sleep that she must not have sex
before marriage or she would go insane. She didn't question
why unmarried mothers were put in asylums; she just
thought, 'Oh well, they deserved it; they'd had sex and
they'd gone mad.'[12]

Is it really any wonder that it is difficult for women to
cope with changes they have helped to produce? Compulsiveness in sexual behaviour, as in other areas, is blunted
autonomy. Given pre-existing sexual orientations, this fact
has different implications for the majority of women, as
compared with most men. For both sexes today, sex carries
with it the promise – or the threat – of intimacy, something
which itself touches upon prime aspects of self. Gerri's
precarious sense of security was deeply connected to her
need repetitively to demonstrate her attractiveness to men.
She was able to obtain sexual pleasure in many of her
encounters but – until the subsequent changes in her life –
withdrew from any longer-term attachments. One could say
that she had internalised a male model of sexuality, tying
sexual experience to a 'quest' built on variety; but, for a
combination of social and psychological reasons, this was a
destructive strategy. As Kasl remarks:

> Very few women set out to have as many sex partners as
> possible. Sexually addicted women get caught up in a cycle
> in which their primary source of power is sexual conquest,
> and they fulfil their need for tenderness and touch through
> the sexual act. Underlying sexually addictive behaviour in
> most women there is a desire for an ongoing relationship.[13]

The sexually compulsive behaviour of women takes various forms, reinforcing the conclusion that it is the underlying syndrome, rather than its specific manifestations, which is important. In some cases compulsive masturbation, perhaps several times a day, is the main element; some such women have few sexual partners. An obsessive preoccupation with sex on the level of fantasy, described by one woman as 'a fear-filled preoccupation with sex',[14] is the dominant feature in other instances. On the part of many, sexual activity resembles the cycle common in eating disorders. A period of frenetic sexual energy alternates with phases in which sex seems repulsive, such that the individual can hardly bear the thought of a further sexual encounter. Most such women appear to be orgasmic. The high of orgasm is a moment of triumph as well as physical and emotional release; but many sustain a high also in the build-up to a sexual encounter, in which they feel peculiarly alert and even euphoric.

Male sexual compulsiveness tends to be different. There is no male equivalent of the loose woman and the sexually adventurous man is often esteemed, particularly among other men. Kasl records that, when she mentioned to a man at a party that she was writing a book on female sex addiction, he reacted in a way that later became very familiar: 'You mean there are women addicted to sex? Hey, I want to meet one of those.'[15] Yet there is much evidence that sexually voracious men do not search out women whose behaviour is close to their own, and are in fact often actively repelled by them. Women are, as ever, divided into two categories so far as the sexual contacts of such men are concerned: those who have to be 'chased' and can therefore be conquered, and those who are in some sense beyond the moral pale and therefore 'do not matter'.[16]

Sex addiction among men is not wholly linked to an obsessive drive for variety. As in the case of women, it may take the form of compulsive masturbation, quite often linked to sexual fantasising that pervades almost all other activities in which the person engages. Occasionally, 'sexaholism' is focused upon one person only. Charlie, described in a study by Susan Forward, reports that he has to have sex with his partner several times a day. His characterisation of his behaviour is reflexively sophisticated, and self-consciously uses the language of addiction: 'We could have had sex ten times that week, but if the eleventh time she'd say "no", I'd feel rejected and get mad at her. I know now it wasn't fair, but all I saw then was that my "fix" was pulling away from me.'[17]

Those who do seek variety, the most driven womanisers, combine a devotion to sexual pursuit with a barely hidden scorn for the very objects of their desire. As one author puts it, 'they pursue women with an urgency and single-mindedness that make ordinary courtship seem casual and desultory and with a recklessness that often jeopardises their marriages, careers and health'.[18] Women who are desired with overwhelming force fade into nothingness as soon as an affair has run its course – although many such men seek stability outside their casual affairs by maintaining a continuous relationship at the same time. In so doing, they often have to go through the most wrenching deceits and cover-ups.

The chase for sexual conquest produces just that deteriorating cycle of despair and disillusionment noted of other addictions. Here is the writer quoted above, speaking of his own experiences, which eventually led him to join a sexual addiction self-help group:

> I realised the measures I had always taken to ward off pain had become themselves immeasurably painful: womanising no longer 'worked' for me. I had lost a great deal in the pursuit of my addiction, and my sense of personal emptiness now overtook me within minutes of my last conquest. Sex no longer gave me anything more than the physical release

of ejaculation; often enough, I simply couldn't reach orgasm. Women were no longer objects of love, or even of desire. I had reached the point where I loathed my partners even as I entered them, and my loathing was all the more because I knew how badly I needed them.[19]

As he goes on to add, it is difficult to accept at face value the claims of some womanisers that their activities are not a problem for them. One man's response to his enquiries was: '*Finding* women is, but womanising, no.' Yet anxiety about, and dread of, women surfaces rapidly in the author's interviews with such men; the calmness with which they might tell of their sexual exploits contrasts with the frenetic nature of the pursuit, and resembles the denial characteristic of other addictions. The remarks with which they gloss their activities are very similar to those used by alcoholics when they justify their drinking: 'it's just this once', 'it doesn't hurt anybody', 'my wife will never find out'.[20]

It is important to make the drift of this discussion clear. Philandering should not be counterposed to an implicit model of monogamy, as if 'fidelity' could be defined in terms of sexual exclusiveness. Womanising is certainly linked to what I shall later call episodic sexuality, but the two are not the same. The connection between them is compulsiveness.

Sexuality and seduction

One might suppose that male sexual compulsiveness is simply male sexuality released from its traditional constraints. After all, haven't there always been many cultures in which rich men have accumulated as many wives or concubines as they can? Isn't Casanova the archetypal male hero – admired also by many women – and the forerunner of the James Bonds of today?

However, the taking of two or more wives, in the context of pre-modern cultures, ordinarily had little or nothing to do with sexual conquest as such. Virtually all polygamous societies have had systems of arranged marriage. Acquiring several wives demanded, and was an expression of, material wealth or social prestige; the same was true of concubinage, where it was an accepted institution. Casanova has no place in pre-modern cultures: he is a figure from a society on the threshold of modernity. He had no interest in accumulating wives, if such a thing were possible. For him, sex was a never-ending search, brought to a conclusion not by the achievement of self-fulfilment or wisdom, but only by the decrepitude of old age. Men want love? Well, certainly in one sense that is precisely the meaning of the life of Casanova. He is the first 'ladies' man', a telling phrase because, appearances to the contrary, it shows who belongs to whom.

Such men love women, although they cannot love any particular woman alone. No doubt it is a love that stems partly from fear but, interestingly, so far as one can tell, Casanova did not have that outright contempt for women that seems so near to the surface among womanisers, as well as at least some gay men, today. He was by no means an exemplary figure: in old age he was reduced to rape as a means of keeping his sexual life going. In his younger days, however, he sought to look after women he had loved and left, and quite often actively arranged suitable husbands for them. Havelock Ellis said of him that he 'loved many women but broke few hearts',[21] although this judgement is certainly over-charitable. Characteristically, in his *Memoirs* Casanova wrote charmingly of the women with whom he became sexually involved, and many of his comments long after the affairs took place were, according to his lights at any rate, generous to and flattering about them.

Casanova was a seducer. His sexual exploits were carried on at a time when unmarried women were supposed to keep themselves virtuous and, among most groups save for the aristocracy, adultery on the part of married women could have devastating consequences if discovered. His seductions had to be managed with care, and were quite often relatively long-term endeavours, as many preparations had to be made. Nor did the process necessarily finish once the conquest had been achieved, since he often had to make sure after the event that a woman's chaperones, guardians or relatives remained unsuspicious.

Womanisers today are the products of the very transformations in personal life that they seem on the face of things to hold out most strongly against. They are seducers in an era in which seduction has virtually become obsolete, and this explains a good deal about the nature of their compulsion. 'Seduction' has lost much of its meaning in a society in which women have become much more sexually 'available' to men than ever before, although – and this is crucial – only as more equal. Womanising reflects this fundamental change at the same time as it grates against it.[22]

Present-day womanisers might appear to be fossils from a previous age, stalking their prey with derring-do, armed only with penicillin, condoms (it is to be hoped) and a preparedness to face the risk of AIDS. Yet if my earlier arguments are correct, womanisers are an intrinsic part of the present-day world of sexuality. They are seducers, yes, and to that extent are concerned above all with sexual conquest and with the exercise of power. But what price victory when victory is so easy? What is there to savour when the other is not only willing, but perhaps equally eager for sexual experience?

The assertion of power in seduction, whereby women are overcome or symbolically 'killed', might seem on the face of things to become all the more challenging when the individual confronts someone who asserts her equality. But female sexual equality, as Graham Hendrick discovered, dissolves the age-old division between the virtuous and the corrupt, or degraded, woman. Since the 'kill' of the seducer depends upon destroying virtue, the pursuit loses its principal dynamic. That 'integrity' which the seducer sought to despoil, or bring within his power, is no longer the same as sexual innocence, and it is no longer gendered. In the context of the pure relationship, integrity retains a fundamental role, but becomes an ethical attribute which each partner presumes of the other.

In more traditional times, the seducer was in his own way a genuine adventurer, throwing down a challenge not just to each woman, but to a whole system of sexual regulation. He was a subverter of virtue and tilted at other windmills too, because seduction meant challenging a male order of sexual protection and control. The womaniser of today is not someone who cultivates sensual pleasure, but a thrill-seeker in a world of open sexual opportunities. The thrill of the pursuit provides the high – but the high tends later to become the fix. Womanisers are not so much libertines as unwitting counter-revolutionaries in an environment in which sexuality and intimacy are tied together as never before. Confluent love presumes intimacy: if such love is not achieved, the individual stands prepared to leave. Womanisers maintain that necessary 'potential space' by means other than respect for the partner. Their ability to 'walk away' is achieved through the anticipation of the next potential sexual encounter. They are often masters of the rhetoric of romantic love, but are unable to produce from it an emotionally coherent narrative of self. Consequently a man who is fluent and assured when going through his seduction routine might find himself awkward, tongue-tied and desperate to get away once the sexual act is over. He is in effect in the position of Karl Krauss's fetishist, who yearns only for a woman's shoe, but instead has to settle for the whole human being.

Some such men have sex with a hundred or more women a year: in what sense could they be said to 'want love'? In a special and urgent sense. Their dependence upon women is obvious enough, so obvious in fact that it is a controlling influence in their lives. Seduction once could easily be assimilated to a male world of achievement and the overcoming of obstacles – the male world of modernity itself. But this orientation becomes empty once seduction loses its earlier meaning. The womaniser cannot be 'special' to each sexual partner in the way in which Casanova could – as the despoiler of virtue but also as a potential rescuer from a life of sexual seclusion. The modern sexual adventurer has rejected romantic love, or uses its language only as persuasive rhetoric. His dependence upon women, therefore, can only be validated through the mechanics of sexual conquest. More than other men, one could argue, the womaniser spots the connections between sexuality, intimacy and the reflexive construction of self-identity; but he is in thrall to women rather than able to meet them as independent beings capable of giving and accepting love. The womaniser appears as a figure who 'loves them and leaves them'. In fact, he is quite unable to 'leave them': each leaving is only a prelude to another encounter.

NOTES

1 Steven Chapple and David Talbot: *Burning Desires*, New York: Signet, 1990, p. 35.
2 There are other organisations and chapters: Sexaholics Anonymous and Sex and Love Addicts Anonymous are mainly heterosexual in orientation; groups such as Sex Compulsives Anonymous are same-sex organisations.
3 Joyce Ditzler and James Ditzler: *If You Really Loved Me. How to Survive an Addiction in the Family*, London: Macmillan, 1989 – just one example of what has become a very extensive literature.
4 Charlotte Kasl: *Women, Sex and Addiction*, London: Mandarin, 1990. Kasl's book is a wonderful resource for considering the

question of sex addiction, and I draw upon it substantially in what follows. Like much of the therapeutic literature I refer to throughout this book, however, I treat it in the manner of Garfinkel's 'documentary method': as a document about personal and social changes in process, but also as symptomatic of them.

5 Ibid., p. 86.
6 Ibid., p. 439.
7 Craig Nakken: *The Addictive Personality. Roots, Rituals and Recovery*, Centre City, Minn.: Hazelden, 1988.
8 Stanton Peele: *Love and Addiction*, New York: New American History, 1975.
9 Erving Goffman: *Interaction Ritual*, London: Allen Lane, 1972.
10 Anthony Giddens: *Modernity and Self-Identity*, Cambridge, Polity, 1991.
11 Ibid.
12 Joy Melville: 'Baby blues', *New Statesman and Society*, 3 May 1991, p. 2.
13 Kasl: *Women, Sex and Addiction*, p. 57.
14 Ibid., p. 58.
15 Ibid., p. 279.
16 Chapple and Talbot: *Burning Desires*, ch. 1.
17 Susan Forward: *Men Who Hate Women and the Women Who Love Them*, New York: Bantam, 1988, p. 68.
18 Peter Trachtenberg: *The Casanova Complex*, New York: Pocket Books, 1988, p. 17.
19 Ibid., p. 289.
20 Ibid., pp. 283–4.
21 Havelock Ellis: *Psychology of Sex*, London: Heinemann, 1946, p. 189.
22 Trachtenberg: *The Casanova Complex*, p. 241.

6

THE SOCIOLOGICAL MEANING OF CODEPENDENCE

Womanisers often have qualities which correlate closely with common traits of the romantic love complex – here are men who will sweep women off their feet, or woo them with particular fervour, and perhaps have become very skilled in so doing. Some women – to whom all those things are by now very familiar – might very well opt for a short-term sexual liaison in the pursuit of transitory excitement or pleasure. For such women the appeal of the lady-killer fades quickly or is deliberately kept in check.

Most lady-killers' ladies are not like this at all.[1] On the contrary, they are likely quite quickly to become deeply involved once any relationship starts up. Such women's lives are strewn with disastrous romances, or long, painful involvements with men who in some way or another abuse them. These women, in short, are codependent, and it has become a commonplace of the therapeutic literature that codependence – although by no means limited to females – is a term that in some ways describes what was once called the 'female role' in general.[2]

Codependent women are carers, who need to give nurturance to others but, partly or almost entirely on an unconscious level, anticipate that their devotion will be rebuffed.

What a painful irony this is! The codependent woman is quite likely to become embroiled in a relationship precisely with a philanderer. She is prepared and perhaps even anxious to 'rescue' him; he requires such tolerance because, unless he is wholly duplicitous, and keeps his real attitudes completely concealed, other women will reject him.

The nature of codependence

The term 'codependent' is an example of that 'reverse reflexivity' so common in the current era. Instead of being coined by professionals, codependence came from the work of individuals struggling with their own alcoholism. In the early alcoholic self-help groups, alcoholism was understood as a weakness of the person affected. It was supposed that the alcoholic recovered best in the company of others suffering from the same problem, away from a family context. Later it came to be recognised that alcoholism affects others with whom the alcoholic is regularly in contact; but most still believed that the alcoholic would have to be cured before being successfully reintegrated into a domestic context. Eventually, however, it became clear that alcoholics have little chance of staying sober if they return to relationships or families where all else remains the same; usually those entire relationships revolve around the alcoholic's addiction.

Others' lives, often in subtle, sometimes in highly damaging, ways, are thus dependent upon the dependency of the addict. One of the first terms coined to interpret this situation was the 'enabler' – the person, usually the sexual partner or spouse, and most commonly a woman, who consciously or unconsciously supports the individual's drinking. The idea of the 'codependent' came to replace that of enabler as it became apparent that such an individual might be suffering as much as, or more than, the person with the chemical dependency.[3]

Once it had become thus generalised, the term 'codependence' was somewhat misleading. It was developed in a context in which there was a clear-cut 'addict', to whose behaviour the other responds. The notion tends to imply a priority in who becomes dependent upon whom; it refers, as it were, to a secondary addiction, the enabler facing the alcoholic. As used in this way, the concept mixes two things: the refraction of an addiction on to another, who builds his or her behaviour around it, and the interactional quality of a relationship. To complicate things further, codependence is quite often linked, not to a specific relationship, but to a type of personality. As one author puts it:

> The codependent seeks approval from practically everyone with whom she comes into contact. Instead of building a life around one person, she may have several 'golden calves' around whom she dances – perhaps her mother and father, her women friends, her boss, and the clerk at the supermarket, in addition to her lover. She lives her life around the needs of others.[4]

Let me formulate the concepts at issue in the following way. A codependent *person* is someone who, in order to sustain a sense of ontological security, requires another individual, or set of individuals, to define her (or his) wants; she or he cannot feel self-confident without being devoted to the needs of others. A codependent *relationship* is one in which an individual is tied psychologically to a partner whose activities are governed by compulsiveness of some sort. I shall term a *fixated* relationship one in which the relationship itself is the object of addiction. In fixated relationships, individuals do not build their lives around the pre-existing addictions of others; rather, they need the relationship to cater to a sense of security which they cannot otherwise meet. In their most benign form, fixated relationships are those entrenched in habit. Such relationships are much more fractious when those concerned are linked through modes of mutual antagonism, from which they are unable to extricate themselves.

We may suppose that fixated relationships are more widespread than codependency in any of its principal forms. A fixated relationship is built around compulsive dependence rather than codependence. Neither party is distinctively an addict, yet both are dependent upon a tie which is either a matter of routinised obligation or actually destructive for the parties concerned. Fixated relationships usually presume role separation. Each person depends upon an 'alterity' which the partner provides; but neither is able fully to recognise, or come to terms with, the nature of his or her dependence upon the other. Men tend to be in fixated relationships in so far as they are with others to whom they are deeply bound, but where that bondedness is either not understood or is actively disclaimed. In the case of women, compulsive dependence is more often associated with a domestic role that has become a fetish – a ritual involvement, for example, with domestic chores and the demands of children.

The work of those who, on the level of therapy, seek to help individuals escape from addictive relationships again provides clues about the structural transformations influencing such relationships. Here once more we encounter the emerging centrality of the pure relationship, as well as its close connections with the reflexive project of self and with a model of confluent love. Addictive ties: 1. do not allow for the monitoring of self and other so vital to the pure relationship; 2. submerge self-identity either in the other or in fixed routines; 3. prevent that opening out to the other which is the precondition of intimacy; 4. tend to preserve inegalitarian gender differences and sexual practices.

The first injunction of all therapy programmes is a reflexive one: recognise that you have a problem and, by dint of that recognition, begin to do something about it! In alcoholic self-help groups, 'bottoming out' is the term often used to describe the state of mind of those who say, 'Enough is enough: I am going to change.' 'Even after the decision has been made at some level, you may still need a jolt to get you to take action. It could be a rejection, a car accident, getting abused by a sexual partner, losing sobriety, or an onslaught of anxiety attacks. Harmful consequences are like a shot of energy to the healthy side.'[5] The decision to take action normally involves securing the help of others outside the addictive relationship itself, for this is a key mode of achieving initial distance as well as support.

The development of reflexive attention entails, as a basic beginning point, the recognition of choice. Choice, it is emphasised, means an appraisal of one's limits and the constraints to which one is subject: this is the way to assess opportunities. The reflexive moment is called by one author 'self talk'. Self talk is a reprogramming, a way of considering how far established routines should be thought of in a new way or, if possible, discarded. Recognition of choice means overcoming 'negative programmes' that support addictive patterns. The following are what addictive programming sounds like:

> 'I just can't do it';
> 'I just know it won't work';
> 'I'm not cut out for that';
> 'I'm not creative enough';
> 'I'll never have enough money';
> 'I can't get along with my boss';
> 'I never seem to have the time I need to get everything done' . . . and so forth.[6]

We should stand back from the naive, almost totalitarian, ring of the injunction to avoid all such thoughts: for, rather

obviously, 'I just can't do it', 'I just know it won't work' and
the rest can often be realistic appraisals of one's opportunities in any given context. Reflexivity is a necessary
condition for emancipation from addiction, not a sufficient
one. None the less, the behavioural importance of such
programming is evident enough.

Choice, it is made clear, reflects directly upon the nature
of the self. What a person wants helps define who that
person is; and finding a secure self-identity is fundamental
to identifying wants. 'There may be a thousand little choices
in a day. All of them count.'[7] But some of them count more
than others. Compulsive relationships, as the therapeutic
literature repeatedly states, although not always in so many
words, preclude the reflexive exploration of self-identity.
Thus a codependent individual is seen by Kasl precisely as
'someone whose core identity is undeveloped or unknown,
and who maintains a false identity built from dependent
attachments to external sources'.[8]

Addiction and the question of intimacy

Codependent individuals are accustomed to finding their
identity through the actions or needs of others; but in any
addictive relationship the self tends to become merged with
the other, because the addiction is a prime source of ontological security. One of the aims often suggested in the early
phases of therapy or self-help groups is that of 'letting go' –
releasing the attempt to control others characteristic of
codependence. The individual is encouraged to try to free
him- or herself from her 'unspoken contract' to put the other
to rights. The process is an extremely difficult one to go
through, although its surface markers are apparent: her
conversations no longer so continually focus upon what 'he'
thinks or does, what 'they' say, 'my husband' or 'my lover'

says. In support groups for the partners of alcoholics, letting go is labelled Loving Detachment, a banal enough phrase for a very real phenomenon – the emerging capability of the codependent to sustain care for the other without shouldering the burden of his or her addiction.[9]

What seems at first blush an encouragement of egoism, even narcissism, should rather be understood as an essential starting-point for the possibility of developing confluent love. It is a prerequisite for recognising the other as an independent being, who can be loved for her or his specific traits and qualities; and also it offers the chance of release from an obsessive involvement with a broken or dying relationship. These are some characteristics, as listed by one therapist, of new habits that might replace the older, more compulsive ones:

You can listen to a friend's problem – just listen – and not try to rescue him or her.

Instead of being focused solely on one person, you are interested in many people.

Instead of returning to the 'scene of the crime' – where your ex-lover lives, or special places the two of you went to – you find more interesting places to visit.

If you desire something or someone who is not available, you enjoy something or someone who is.

Instead of putting up with abuse, you say no to the relationship.

If you have just broken up with a lover, and he always called at a certain time, you find another pleasurable pursuit to do at that time.[10]

Defining personal boundaries is regarded as fundamental for a non-addictive relationship. Why? The answer again directly concerns the self and its reflexivity. Boundaries establish what belongs to whom, psychologically speaking, and thereby counteract the effects of projective identification. Clear boundaries within a relationship are obviously important for confluent love and the sustaining of intimacy. Intimacy is not being absorbed by the other, but knowing his or her characteristics and making available one's own. Opening out to the other, paradoxically, requires personal boundaries, because it is a communicative phenomenon; it also requires sensitivity and tact, since it is not the same as living with no private thoughts at all. The balance of openness, vulnerability and trust developed in a relationship governs whether or not personal boundaries become divisions which obstruct rather than encourage such communication.[11]

This balance also presumes a balance of power – which is why the pure relationship, with its promise of intimacy, depends both upon the increasing autonomy of women and upon plastic sexuality, no longer harnessed to the double standard. The same therapist mentioned above provides a chart identifying characteristics of addictive versus intimate relationships:

Addictive	Intimate
Obsession with finding 'someone to love'	Development of self as a first priority
Need for immediate gratification	Desire for long-term contentment; relationship develops step by step
Pressuring partner for sex or commitment	Freedom of choice
Imbalance of power	Balance and mutuality in the relationship
Power plays for control	Compromise, negotiation or taking turns at leading
No-talk rule, especially if things are not working out	Sharing wants, feelings, and appreciation of what your partner means to you

Manipulation	Directness
Lack of trust	Appropriate trust (that is, knowing that your partner will probably behave according to his or her fundamental nature)
Attempts to change partner to meet one's needs	Embracing of each other's individuality
Relationship is based on delusion and avoidance of the unpleasant	Relationship deals with all aspects of reality
Relationship is always the same	Relationship is always changing
Expectation that one partner will fix and rescue the other	Self-care by both partners
Fusion (being obsessed with each other's problems and feelings)	Loving detachment (healthy concern about partner's well-being and growth, while letting go)
Passion confused with fear	Sex grows out of friendship and caring
Blaming self or partner for problems	Problem-solving together
Cycle of pain and despair	Cycle of comfort and contentment[12]

Pious psychobabble? Perhaps, at least to some degree. Self-contradictory, in respect of some of the claims made in the right-hand column? Undoubtedly – although to some extent these express real contradictions of personal life. Yet I do not think the possibilities listed are mere wishful thinking; they reflect some of the tendential characteristics of the transformation of intimacy which I seek to document throughout the book. Who could fail to see in them evidence of, and a programme for, the democratisation of daily life? Comparing the list on the left-hand side with that on the right reveals a picture of emancipation. This is not just a 'freeing from': as portrayed here intimacy has a substantive content. We begin to see what a liberated personal domain might look like.

Intimacy, kinship, parenthood

The transformation of intimacy is about sex and gender, but it is not limited to them – a fact which supports the thesis, which I shall develop in some detail later, that what is at issue here is a basic transition in the ethics of personal life as a whole. Like gender, kinship was once seen as naturally given, a series of rights and obligations which biological and marriage ties created. Kinship relations, it has been widely argued, have been largely destroyed with the development of modern institutions, which have left the nuclear family standing in splendid isolation. Without taking up the question in any detail, it can be seen that this view is mistaken, or at least misleading. In the separating and divorcing society, the nuclear family generates a diversity of new kin ties associated, for example, with so-called recombinant families. However, the nature of these ties changes as they are subject to greater negotiation than before. Kinship relations often used to be a taken for granted basis of trust; now trust has to be negotiated and bargained for, and commitment is as much of an issue as in sexual relationships.

Janet Finch speaks of a process of 'working out' when analysing kinship relations today.[13] People have to work out how to treat relatives and, in so doing, construct novel ethics of day-to-day life. She treats this process explicitly in terms of a language of commitment. People tend to organise their kinship connections through 'negotiated commitment', whereby they work out the 'proper thing to do' for their relatives in a specific range of contexts. For instance, an individual does not decide to lend money to a brother-in-law because this is defined in the family or wider society as an obligation; rather the money is lent because the person has developed a series of commitments to the other which defines it as the right thing to do.

How far do the relations between parents and children differ from this situation? Evidently in adult–child interaction there is a marked imbalance of power, especially in the early years of the life of the child. In the light of this fact, one might suppose that the quality of the relationship has little bearing upon the care provided, since there are pre-given social obligations of a binding kind on both sides. Yet there is good reason to doubt how strong such obligations are among many groups today. The best way to demonstrate this is to work 'backwards' from parent–child ties that are clearly negotiated to those characteristic of early childhood. Many parents are now step-parents as well as biological mothers and fathers. Step-parents usually accept some obligations towards, and rights over, children, but these are today generally 'negotiated commitments' in Finch's sense, from the side of the children as well as the adults. Or take the case of the obligations adult children assume towards ageing parents. In some circumstances and cultural contexts it is more or less taken for granted that the parents can count on their children for material and social support. But the clear trend of development is for such support to depend upon the quality of relationships forged.

The determining influence seems to be what could be described as the forming of cumulative commitments.[14] In a study of mothers and daughters, for example, one respondent says, 'My mother and I lived together because we chose to, we liked each other . . . we shared a common home, we could laugh together . . . I was an independent person, so was my mother. We were living together, I wasn't just looking after her.'[15] She felt a commitment to care for her mother, as a result of their long history together; but the element of mutual liking was important. As Finch points out, the notion of cumulative commitments helps us to understand how, over a period of time, it becomes 'obvious' to one sibling that various forms of care should be provided for one or both parents, whereas another might feel quite differently.[16]

The picture is more complex in the case of the relation of parents to younger children. Not only are parents much more powerful than very young children; their attitudes and conduct shape the child's personality and dispositions. Yet it would certainly not be right to suppose that childhood has remained unaffected by the world of pure relationships. The social invention of motherhood presaged, and gave concrete form to, the idea that the mother should develop an affectionate relationship with the child, one that gives specific weight to the child's needs. Child-rearing manuals published in the early part of the current century advised parents not to become too friendly with their children on the grounds that their authority would become weakened. Later the view developed that parents should seek to foster close emotional ties with their children, but also give due recognition to the child's autonomy.[17] Just as some have spoken of narcissism to refer to the position of the self in modern society, others have suggested that parent–child interaction has moved towards greater 'permissiveness'. But this is an inadequate label to refer to the endeavour to develop alternative child-rearing strategies to those of the past. It is the quality of the relationship which comes to the fore, with a stress upon intimacy replacing that of parental authoritativeness. Sensitivity and understanding are asked for on both sides.[18]

Parents and children

In therapeutic discussions of codependent or fixated relationships, almost without exception, individuals who wish to develop close personal ties with others are advised to 'heal the child within'. The relations between parents and young children here reappear in a fundamental way as relevant to the pure relationship and the model of confluent love. Why is a 'release from the past' so important for the attainment of intimacy? Since so many forms of therapy, beginning with psychoanalysis, are oriented to childhood experience, answering this question might very well provide further clues to the significance of therapy and counselling in modern culture in general.

We can again start out with a therapeutic guide, in this instance Susan Forward, as she gives advice about how to 'heal the past'.[19] Her discussion concentrates upon the case of Nicki, a young woman who was experiencing difficulties in her marriage. She was unable to stand up for herself in the relationship, and when her husband was angry with her she felt humiliated and defenceless. The therapist asked her to recall incidents in her childhood that had made her feel a similar way, and came up with a particular example – one of those incidents that sticks permanently in the mind. Her father always wanted her to learn to play the piano well, and although she herself wasn't very interested, she tried hard in order to please him. When she played in front of other people, she became anxious and the level of her performance deteriorated. At one recital she was so nervous that she left out a whole section of the piece she was asked to play. On the way home from the recital her father told her that, after her débâcle, he didn't know how he would ever be able to look any of the audience in the face again. She had disgraced him in front of everyone, was thoughtless, careless and too lazy to practise.

She had felt utterly crushed, having wanted so much to please him. In her words, 'I just felt like dying.' The therapist perceived that in her marriage she was re-enacting scenes from her childhood and 'losing her adult self'.[20] She asked Nicki to bring in a picture of herself as a little girl, and when they looked at the photo together Nicki remembered many other circumstances in which her father had shamed her in a similar way. Forward then suggested that she go down to the local school and spot a girl who reminded her of herself at the same age. The idea was that she should imagine that girl being humiliated in the same manner as she felt she had been; in such a way she could realise how small and defenceless she was at the time when the original event happened. It was this 'child within' who became so fearful and timid when her husband criticised her.

Nicki was later asked by the therapist to imagine that her father was sitting in an empty chair in front of her, and to say to him the things she'd always wanted to say, but was never able to do. Trembling with anger, she shouted:

> How dare you treat me like that! How dare you humiliate me the way you did! Who the hell did you think you were? I always looked up to you. I worshipped you. Couldn't you tell how much you were hurting me? Nothing I ever did was good enough for you. You made me feel like a total failure, you bastard. I would have done anything for you, just to get you to love me a little.[21]

Unfair to fathers, the reader – or at least the male reader – might be tempted to say. For perhaps, after all, he was doing his best. Yet this is not the point, for whatever he intended, she felt an enduring shame. According to Forward, this and other therapeutic exercises were of great value in siphoning off the accumulated rage Nicki harboured against her father.

She was asked to make an inventory of all the negative

things her father, in her eyes, had felt about her. She came up with a long list:

I am inconsiderate
I am selfish
I am thoughtless
I am talentless
I am inadequate
I am an embarrassment to my family
I am disappointing
I am ungrateful
I am a bad person
I am a failure
I am shiftless
I am lazy and will never amount to anything.

She immediately saw that she had taken over many of these opinions about herself; and she went back to the list she had written out and wrote in a bold hand, 'It wasn't true then and it isn't true now!' In contrast to her views of her father, she felt that her mother had always been loving and supportive. This is a list of what she saw as her mother's positive opinions of her:

I am intelligent
I am sweet
I am charming
I am generous
I am talented
I am a hard worker
I am good-natured
I am full of energy
I am lovable
I am a joy to have around.[22]

After she had written this list, Nicki scrawled across it: 'This is true and it always has been.' She later came to accept that her parents' views of her had not been as polarised as she had always assumed. Her father, for example, had quite often complimented her on her intelligence, looks and athletic abilities. She gradually learned to 'reparent the little child within her' and dispel the internal image of the critical father. Whether Nicki was able effectively to improve her relationship with her father, whom she saw infrequently, Forward does not say. She came eventually to abandon her fantasy that her father would ever be 'the father I always wanted'. There was 'grief and mourning' in so doing, but 'also a great deal of freedom. All the energy she had spent in a fruitless search for her father's love could now be used in the pursuit of activities that were positive and meaningful to her.'[23]

I am not concerned with how far these particular techniques of therapy are effective compared with, say, classical psychoanalysis or other therapies which focus in a more subtle way on the unconscious. Fostering the 'child within' means retrieving the past – a process of going back, and recapturing half-remembered or repressed childhood experiences – but only in order to release it. The emphasis is upon the present and the future, and the severity of the break with the past is indicated by the fact that a mourning process is required to give it up. Are we talking here of yet another addiction which needs to be broken? In a looser sense of the term than that discussed previously, I think we are. The therapist is encouraging Nicki to 'let go' of traits which, destructive as they were, had something of a compulsive grip upon her attitudes and actions.

The significance of mourning pervades a great deal of the therapeutic literature. Consider, for instance, the analysis of 'loveshock' offered by Stephen Gullo and Connie Church.[24] Gullo developed the idea of loveshock from therapeutic work he carried out with Vietnam veterans suffering from battle fatigue, often more popularly known as shell-shock.[25] Soldiers returning from Vietnam suffered from psychological disorientation, numbness of feelings and an incapacity to form close relationships with anyone save their old battlefield comrades. Gullo noticed parallels between the experiences of the soldiers and the reactions of people when serious love relationships ended. The comparison might seem to trivialise the distress produced by battle fatigue, but in fact the intensity of the reactions to the breakup of an established relationship is sometimes almost as great, and recovery as prolonged.

When a relationship ends, even for one who is the 'rejector' rather than the person abandoned, an image of the other, habits associated with the other and the expectation that a reconciliation may take place may persist for many years afterwards. Mourning is the condition of letting go of habits which otherwise translate themselves into addictive traits in the present. Loveshock has a 'psychological travelling time', which may take a period of many months to work through, although how long it lasts varies according to the degree of emotional involvement with the memories which the individual must rework. Becoming resigned to the break, 'bidding goodbye', is normally only achieved in the later stages of withdrawal, once grief and blame have substantially been dealt with.

It is not fanciful to compare letting go in dissolved adult relationships with the effort to free an adult, such as Nicki, from a compulsive involvement with childhood events and traumas. In each case there is a cognitive and emotional coming to terms with the psychological past, and a rewriting of the narrative of self. In both instances a failure to 'break away' is likely to mean the repetition of similar patterns of behaviour, forming a cycle rather than a path of autonomous self-development. 'Confronting your loveshock experience and learning from what went wrong in the relationship can turn the pain into a growth experience and provide you with insights and coping skills that can enhance your next relationship.'[26]

In speaking of the relations between adult children and their parents, it needs an effort of the imagination to think in terms of 'recovery' in the way which comes quite naturally when one considers the situation of someone getting over the loss of a loved partner. Childhood seems to be something that prepares one for later, more autonomous, participation in an adult world rather than a phase of life from which, as an adult, one must seek to escape. Yet the parent–child relationship, like others, is one from which the individual has to break free, although not normally because it disintegrates in the same way as an adult love relationship. Suppose we took the unusual step of treating parent–child involvement as just one relationship among others which individuals form and from which they move out. It immediately becomes apparent that many parent–child relationships would be regarded, from a therapeutic point of view, as severely defective – if the children were not intrinsically dependent upon their parents, one would expect them to leave. As I shall try to indicate, some interesting conclusions follow if we see 'badly behaved' parents in the same way as we would spouses who regularly trample on the other's needs.

Toxic parents?

Let me follow through further the therapeutic work of Susan Forward as she generalises her concerns with Nicki to offer a full-blown account of the conditions under which parents can prove 'toxic' for their children.[27] What is a toxic parent? There is a well-known saying to the effect that however parents behave towards their children it will be wrong; no parent can discern all of a child's needs or adequately respond to them. Yet there are many parents who consistently treat their children in a manner that damages their sense of personal worth – and might cause them to engage in life-long battles with the memories and figures of their childhood. Toxic parents

> tend to see rebellion or even individual differences as a personal attack. They defend themselves by reinforcing their child's dependence and helplessness. Instead of promoting healthy development, they unconsciously undermine it, often with the belief that they are acting in their child's best interest. They may use such phrases as 'it builds character' or 'she needs to learn right from wrong', but their arsenals of negativity really harm their child's self-esteem, sabotaging any budding independence . . . At the core of every formerly mistreated adult – even high achievers – is a little child who feels powerless and afraid.[28]

Forward identifies a whole variety of toxic parents. There are parents who are simply 'emotionally inadequate'. They are not 'there' for their children, who may as a result feel they have to protect them, or may strive endlessly to find tokens of their love. These are parents who, whether intentionally or not, have abdicated their responsibilities to their children. A different category of toxic parents are controllers. The feelings and needs of the children are subordinated to those of the parents. The typical reaction of children brought up in this way is, 'Why can't they let me live my own life?'

These types of parental toxicity are relatively subtle; others are more directly brutalising. Alcoholism again features in an important way. In most families in which one or both parents are addicted to alcohol, a systematic cover-up of that fact is made, with which the children are in effect asked to collude, often producing crippling effects on their own personal development. 'No one in this family is alcoholic' is the image offered to the outside world, but inside the family group the pressures placed on the children can be overwhelming.

Then there are verbal and physical abusers. All parents at times say things which their children find hurtful; but if that hurt is visible perhaps most will try to repair the damage with kindness or an apology. Yet some parents assail their children with more or less constant sarcasm, insults or name-calling. 'If someone turned you inside out, they'd see stink coming out of every pore in your body', the father of one of Forward's clients said to his daughter; he made a point of often telling her how badly she smelled.[29]

Regular verbal abuse quite frequently goes along with the physical beating of children. Physical abuse is defined in US federal law as 'the infliction of physical injuries such as bruises, burns, welts, cuts, bone and skull fractures; these are caused by kicking, punching, biting, beating, knifing, strapping, paddling, etc.'. Legal provisions against the physical punishment of children, in the United States as in other countries, are usually only invoked in extreme cases of parental violence, and many such instances never come to the attention of the police. Children whose parents are indifferent to them might batter them as a means of expressing other frustrations; but of course the injunction 'don't spare the rod' is often followed by parents who believe that physical discipline is a necessary part of inducing respect for authority.

Finally, there is parental sexual abuse, that phenomenon which, as we now know, in its various guises affects substantial proportions of children, both female and male. Incest has come to be understood not just as a secret wish, but as a reality in very many families, stretching across all social classes. Even when defined quite narrowly, to exclude visual and verbal sexual harassment, and include only the direct stimulation of the erogenous zones of the body, incest is vastly more common than once was generally thought by welfare professionals and specialists in the study of the family. Research suggests that some 5 per cent of all children under the age of eighteen have at some point been sexually molested by one or other parent (including step-parents).[30] The level of sexual abuse if other family members are taken into account is much higher. Most, but not all, is carried out by men; unlike rape, sexual abuse of children is not exclusively a male crime. Boys seem almost as often the victims of incest as girls; father–son incest is easily the most frequently found type, but the sexual molesting of sons by mothers is not uncommon.

Toxic parents: aren't we speaking here of ways in which many parents have long behaved towards their children, especially if we have in mind the less extreme and invasive forms of abuse? In some substantial part I think such is the case. The period during which family size declined, and children became more 'valued' by parents, was one in which the idea that children should obey their elders and betters took root. Yet even at its inception this was a notion ready to be subverted by the creation of an expanding sphere of intimacy – and it was also largely a male doctrine, upheld by the rule of the father. The dicipline of the father tied the child to tradition, to a particular interpretation of the past; authority in this situation remained largely dogmatic assertion, backed in many instances by physical punishment. Partly as a result of the 'creation of motherhood', a softer and more egalitarian form of child-rearing emerged, in which more autonomy was accorded to the child. The stage today is set for a further transition: the translation of the child's ties to its parents – as well as to others in the family – into a relationship in the contemporary sense of that term.

Consider some of the advice Forward gives for those who wish to rework their involvements with toxic parents. Even though this may take a lengthy period of therapy, the person has to come to learn two overriding principles: 'You are *not* responsible for what was done to you as a defenceless child!'

and 'You *are* responsible for taking positive steps to do something about it now!' How might these things be achieved? The individual is recommended first of all to seek to attain a measure of emotional independence from his or her parents. She or he must learn to 'respond' rather than merely 'react' in an automatic way to parental behaviour – even where the interaction is with memories of a parent or parents rather than with living beings. As part of this process, the therapist advises that the person starts to say 'I can't', 'I won't' in relation to real or hypothetical parental demands – as a way of asserting autonomy. Subsequently, the aim is to re-evaluate the terms upon which the parent–child interaction is based, such that all parties can as far as possible treat each other as equals. 'I can't', 'I won't', then becomes, not just a blocking-off device, but a negotiated standpoint in terms of which the individual is able to exercise choice. For 'lack of choice is directly connected to enmeshment'.[31]

At this point we can pull together some threads running through this entire chapter. The issue of toxic parents allows clear insight into the connections between the reflexive project of self, the pure relationship and the emergence of new ethical programmes for the restructuring of personal life. Declaring 'emotional independence' from one's parents is a means of simultaneously beginning to reform the narrative of self and making an assertion about one's rights (as well as leading to a reasoned acceptance of responsibilities). The individual's behaviour is no longer organised in terms of a compulsive re-enactment of childhood routines. There is a direct parallel here with the overcoming of addictions formed in later life, which themselves ordinarily stem from habits established at a much earlier stage.

A toxic parental background prevents the individual from developing a narrative of self understood as a 'biographical accounting' with which she or he feels emotionally comfortable. Lack of self-esteem, which usually takes the form of unconscious or unacknowledged shame, is one important consequence; even more basic is the individual's incapacity to approach other adults as emotional equals. Escaping from toxic parental backgrounds is inseparable from the assertion of certain ethical principles or rights. Individuals who seek to alter their relationship to their parents by means of looking back to childhood experience are in effect claiming rights. Children have rights not just to be fed, clothed and protected but rights to be cared for emotionally, to have their feelings respected and their views and feelings taken into account. In short, the characteristics of confluent love appropriate to adult relationships are no less relevant to relations between adults and children.

For people when they *are* children, especially tiny children not yet able verbally to articulate needs, assertions of rights are counterfactual. They have to be made by adults, on the level of ethical arguments. This observation helps illuminate the issue of authority. As parent–child ties approximate more and more to the pure relationship, it might seem that the outlook of the parent has no primacy over the inclinations of the child – resulting in a 'permissiveness' run riot. But this does not follow at all. A liberalising of the personal sphere would not mean the disappearance of authority; rather, coercive power gives way to authority relations which can be defended in a principled fashion. This issue I shall discuss at greater length in the concluding chapter.

NOTES

1 Peter Trachtenberg: *The Casanova Complex*, New York: Pocket Books, 1988, pp. 244–8.
2 Cf., for example, Colette Dowling: *The Cinderella Complex*, New York: Pocket Books, 1981, p. 34.
3 Anne Wilson Schaeff: *Codependence. Misunderstood-Mistreated*, San Francisco: Harper and Row, 1986, p. 11.

4 Jody Hayes: *Smart Love*, London: Arrow, 1990, p. 31.
5 Charlotte Kasl: *Women, Sex and Addiction*, London: Mandarin, 1990, p. 340.
6 Shad Helmstetter: *Choices*, New York: Pocket Books, 1989, p. 47.
7 Ibid., p. 97.
8 Kasl: *Women, Sex and Addiction*, p. 36.
9 Hayes: *Smart Love*, pp. 63–4.
10 Ibid., p. 73.
11 C. Edward Crowther: *Intimacy. Strategies for Successful Relationships*, New York: Dell, 1988, pp. 156–8.
12 Hayes: *Smart Love*, pp. 174–5.
13 Janet Finch: *Family Obligations and Social Change*, Cambridge: Polity, 1989, pp. 194–211.
14 Ibid., pp. 204–5.
15 J. Lewis and B. Meredith: *Daughters Who Care*, London: Routledge, 1988, p. 54.
16 Finch: *Family Obligations and Social Change*, p. 205.
17 H. Gadlin: 'Child discipline and the pursuit of the self: an historical interpretation', *Advances in Child Development and Behaviour*, vol. 12, 1978.
18 Ibid., pp. 75–82.
19 Susan Forward: *Men Who Hate Women and the Women Who Love Them*, New York: Bantam, 1988.
20 Ibid., p. 193.
21 Ibid., p. 195.
22 Ibid., pp. 198–9.
23 Ibid., p. 202.
24 Stephen Gullo and Connie Church: *Loveshock. How to Recover from a Broken Heart and Love Again*, London: Simon and Schuster, 1989.
25 For the classical study of the psychological implications of battle fatigue, see William Sargant: *Battle for the Mind*, London: Pan, 1959.
26 Gullo and Church: *Loveshock*, p. 28.
27 Susan Forward: *Toxic Parents. Overcoming Their Hurtful Legacy and Reclaiming Your Life*, New York: Bantam, 1990.
28 Ibid., p. 16.
29 Ibid., pp. 106–7.
30 David Finkelhor et al.: *The Dark Side of Families*, Beverley Hills: Sage, 1983.
31 Forward: *Toxic Parents*, p. 211.

7

PERSONAL TURBULENCE, SEXUAL TROUBLES

It has been remarked that 'in all the voluminous literature on sex and sexuality, there is very little on male sexuality as such . . . It seems as if it's so much an accepted part of everyday life that it is invisible.'[1] An eccentric judgement, one might think, given the preoccupation of Freud, and many who came after him, with male sexual experience. Yet if understood, not in terms of sexual activity itself, but in relation to the sentiments and conflicts which sex arouses, the observation makes some sense.

Male sexuality appeared unproblematic in the context of the 'seperate and unequal' social circumstances that prevailed until recently. Its nature was concealed by a range of social influences, all of which have now been, or are being, undermined. They include the following: 1. the domination of men over the public sphere; 2. the double standard; 3. the associated schism of women into pure (marriageable) and impure (prostitutes, harlots, concubines, witches); 4. the understanding of sexual difference as given by God, nature or biology; 5. the problematising of women as opaque or irrational in their desires and actions; 6. the sexual division of labour.

The more these pre-existing social forms become dissolved – although all still have a hold – the more we should expect male sexuality to become troubled and, very often,

compulsive. Male sexual compulsiveness can be understood, as a previous chapter indicated, as an obsessive, but
brittle, acting out of routines that have become detached
from their erstwhile supports. It forms an 'odyssey' comparable to that of modernity itself, viewed at least from the
domain of its public institutions – one which is concerned
with control and emotional distance, but which is edged
with potential violence.

Sexuality and psychoanalytic theory: preliminary comments

Freud's discovery of plastic sexuality – documented in his
Three Essays – an extraordinary achievement, sits uneasily
with his interpretation of male, as well as female, sexual
development. For that development, as Freud describes it,
is predicated upon a 'natural' sequence in which erotic
energies are directed towards specific objects in the child's
environment. If we place an emphasis upon plastic sexuality, and ask just why girls should be envious of boys, rather
than taking for granted envy based upon a given physical
quality, we can begin to reconstruct the origins of 'maleness'
in a different way from Freud himself.

The Oedipal transition, the cornerstone of Freud's mature
analysis of psychosexual development, does not appear in a
significant way in *Three Essays*. When that work was written
the theory of the Oedipus complex had only been formulated in a rudimentary fashion. Thus although Freud later
modified the arguments of the *Three Essays* in the light of his
subsequent views, the ideas that sexuality has no intrinsic
object and that male and female sexuality are functionally
equivalent ceded place to the assumption of maleness and
male sexuality as the norm. Boys have the advantage that
their genitals are visible and are more easily localised as the

source of erotic stimulation. Sexual development is a threat-ening affair for boys just as it is for girls: being visible, the penis is also vulnerable, and the rivalry of the boy with his father is the basis of an extremely tensionful mixture of loss and the achievement of autonomy. Yet the little girl is a deprived being in a more profound sense, for her visible inadequacy is intrinsic to her existence. She is dispossessed from the start, because she was born 'castrated'; her hetero-sexuality is gained only in a secondary way, as she learns she can never possess the mother since she lacks a penis. There is no direct route to femininity.

Given the prominence of his notion of penis envy, Freud's writings seem unpromising as a source of inspiration for feminist authors. In fact, the encounter between feminism and psychoanalysis has proved to be the source of important and original contributions to psychological and social theory.[2] A major division, however, has developed between the work of authors – Julia Kristeva, Luce Irigaray and others – influenced by Jacques Lacan and by the philosoph-ical perspective of post-structuralism, and those – such as Nancy Chodorow, Dorothy Dinnerstein or Carol Gilligan – more under the sway of the object-relations school. The differences between these standpoints is in one sense pro-found, but in another sense can be exaggerated. The less important factor is that which seems on the face of things the most significant: the impact of post-structuralism.

I hope the reader unfamiliar with the debates on these matters will forgive a lapse into a rather more demanding vocabulary over the next two or three paragraphs than I have sought to use in the rest of the text. According to post-structuralist thought, nothing has an essence; everything is structured in the mobile play of signifiers. As refracted through the feminist debate with and use of Freud, this standpoint becomes expressed as a critique of 'essentialism'. If meanings are always defined negatively, through what they are not, then 'sexual identity', or 'self-identity' more generally, are misnomers: they imply a spurious unity. Such a view finds further support in the Lacanian contention of the 'splitting': the subject only shows itself through misrecognition.

The critique of 'essentialism', in my opinion at any rate, is based upon a misplaced theory of language.[3] Meaning is defined through difference, certainly; not in an endless play of signifiers, but in pragmatic contexts of use. There is absolutely no reason why, on the level of logic, acknowledgement of the context-dependent nature of language dissolves continuity of identity. The question of 'essentialism' is a red herring, save as an empirical issue of how far self-identity is tenuous or fragmentary and of how far there are generic qualities which tend to distinguish men from women.

More consequential is the status of the Lacanian thesis, appropriated by at least some feminist authors, that women are specifically excluded from the domain of the symbolic, of language as such. For Irigaray, for example, whatever her other criticisms of Lacan, there is no signifying economy for the feminine: femininity is a 'hole' in a double sense. This position, however, is an artefact of the connection Lacan draws between the symbolic and the 'law of the father', which there seems no good reason to accept. More plausible to suggest, with Chodorow, that 'male language', in so far as it exists, tends to be more instrumental and theoretical than that of women – but that, in some key respects, 'male language' expresses deprivation just as much as dominance. In my discussion here, therefore, I shall draw upon the object-relations approach rather than the Lacanian one. Some of the emphases of Lacanian feminist theory, nevertheless, need to be borne in mind – particularly its insistence upon the fragmentary and contradictory character of sexual identity. Once the post-structuralist lens is cast aside, there is no reason why such emphases cannot be sustained in the context of an object-relations perspective.

Psychosocial development and male sexuality

Following Chodorow, one can affirm that, in the first years of life – particularly and perhaps *only* in contemporary society – the influence of the mother overrides that of the father and other caretakers.[4] The early experience the child has of the mother is virtually the opposite of the image of a castrated and impotent individual; particularly on an unconscious level, the little boy, and girl, see the mother as all-powerful. An early sense of self-identity, then, together with the potential for intimacy, is first of all developed through identification with a pervasively important female figure. To achieve a consolidated sense of independence, all children must at some point begin to free themselves from the mother's influence and thus disengage from her love. It follows that it is the route to masculinity, rather than to femininity, which is a detour. The origins of male self-identity are bound up with a deep sense of insecurity, a sense of loss that haunts the individual's unconscious memories thereafter. Basic trust, the very source of ontological security, is intrinsically compromised, since the boy is abandoned to the world of men by the very person who was the main loved adult upon whom he could count.

From this point of view, for both sexes the phallus, that imaginary representation of the penis, derives its meaning from the fantasy of female dominance.[5] It symbolises separation, but also revolt and freedom. In the phase before the Oedipal transition, phallic power comes more from the separation of the spheres of authority of the mother and father than from sheer male preeminence as such. The phallus represents freedom from overwhelming dependence upon the mother as well as the capacity to pull back from her love and attention; it is a key symbol in the child's early search for an independent self-identity. Penis envy, a real phenomenon, as Jessica Benjamin argues, represents the wish of young children, boys and girls, to identify with the father, as the prime representative of the outside world.[6] The Oedipal phase, when it arrives, confirms the boy's separation from the mother, but offers the reward of greater freedom – or rather, wilfulness, which is not exactly the same thing – in exchange. Masculinity is thus energetic and striving, yet the energy of the boy covers over a primal loss.

The more the transformation of intimacy proceeds, on an institutional level, the more the Oedipal transition tends to be connected to 'rapprochement': the ability of parents and children to interact on the basis of an understanding of the other's rights and the other's emotions. The question of the 'absent father', first brought up by the Frankfurt School and more recently by male activist groups, can here be seen in a positive rather than a negative light. Less a specifically disciplining figure, because much early discipline is in any case taken over by the mother, the father (or the idealised father figure) has become, in Hans Leowald's terms, more 'generous'.[7] We find here an intrusion of shame into the development of the male psyche, although, compared with girls, guilt still has a prominent place. At stake is not so much identification with a distinctly punitive figure as a defensive repudiation of nurturance.

The masculine sense of self-identity is thus forged in circumstances in which a drive to self-sufficiency is coupled with a potentially crippling emotional handicap. A narrative of self-identity has to be developed which writes out the pain of the deprivation of early mother-love. No doubt elements of all this are more or less universal, but what is important in the current context is the peculiarly tensionful outcome for male sexuality in a situation where mother-love – if indeed, it is received at all – is simultaneously all-important and forgone. The penis is the phallus, yes, but today in circumstances in which the sustaining of phallic power becomes increasingly focused upon the penis, or rather, genital sexuality, as its main expression.

Understanding masculinity, in modern societies, in this way helps illuminate the typical forms of male sexual compulsiveness. Many men are driven, by means of their scrutiny of women, to search for what is lacking in themselves – and this is a lack that can manifest itself in overt rage and violence. It has become a commonplace in the therapeutic literature to say that men tend to be 'unable to express feelings' or are 'out of touch' with their own emotions. But this is much too crude. Instead, we should say that many men are unable to construct a narrative of self that allows them to come to terms with an increasingly democratised and reordered sphere of personal life.

Male sexuality, compulsiveness, pornography

The frangible nature of male sexuality in modern social circumstances is well documented in contemporary therapeutic case-studies. Heather Formani remarks that 'whatever masculinity is, it is very damaging to men', and the case-study material she discusses provides ample justification for this observation.[8] Compared with women, more men tend to be sexually restless; yet they also compartmentalise their sexual activity from the parts of their lives in which they are able to find stability and integrity of direction.[9]

The compulsive character of the drive towards episodic sexuality becomes greater in so far as women locate, and reject, their complicity with the hidden emotional dependence of the male. Romantic love, as I have tried to show, always carried within it a protest about such complicity, although in some ways it helped support it. The more women press towards an ethics of confluent love, the more male emotional dependence becomes untenable; but the more difficult it may be for many men to deal with the moral nakedness which this implies. To the degree to which the phallus actually becomes the penis, male sexuality is liable to be torn between assertive sexual dominance, including the use of violence, on the one hand, and constant anxieties about potency on the other (which are likely to surface most often in relationships of some duration, where sexual performance cannot be isolated from emotional involvements of various kinds).

Male anxiety about sexuality was largely hidden from view so long as the various social conditions that protected it, noted above, were in place. If women's capacity and need for sexual expression were kept carefully under wraps until well into the twentieth century, so also was the concurrent traumatising of the male. Lesley Hall's analysis of letters written by men to Marie Stopes illustrates this vein of sexual inquietude and despair – which is as far from the image of the carefree lecher or impetuous, unbridled sexuality as one can get.[10] Impotence, nocturnal emissions, premature ejaculation, worries about penis size and function – these and other anxieties occur again and again in the letters. Many of the men who contacted Stopes took good care to point out that they were not weaklings, but 'a big man and strong', 'above the average in physical fitness', 'well-built, athletic, physically very strong' and so forth.

Anxiety based on lack of knowledge about sex is a persistent theme, as are chronic sentiments of inferiority and personal confusion. Inability to generate sexual responsiveness in the partner is a common complaint, but so is lack of pleasure on the part of the man. 'Neither of us ever feels that satisfaction in the closest embrace which instinct and reason tell me should be the case', as one individual expressed it.[11] Most of the sexual worries Stopes's correspondents felt centred upon either sexual failure or worries about normality; failures in 'manhood' were experienced as threats to a valued relationship, rather than problems expressed in the abstract.

Although I make no pretence to discussing such issues in detail, the foregoing analysis helps make sense both of certain features of mass pornography and important aspects of male sexual violence. Pornography might be regarded as the commodifying of sex, but this would be a very partial view. The current explosion of pornographic material, much of which is primarily directed at men, and for the most part is exclusively consumed by them, closely parallels in form the prevalent concentration upon low emotion, high intensity sex. Heterosexual pornography displays an obsessive concern with standardised scenes and poses in which the complicity of women, substantially dissolved in the actual social world, is reiterated in an unambiguous way.[12] The images of women in soft pornographic magazines – normalised by their insertion in orthodox advertising, non-sexual stories and news items – are objects of desire, but never love. They excite and stimulate and, of course, they are quintessentially episodic.

Female complicity is portrayed in the stylised manner in which women are usually depicted. The 'respectability' of soft pornography is an important part of its appeal, carrying the implication as it does that women are the objects, but not the subjects, of sexual desire. In the visual content of pornographic magazines, female sexuality is neutralised, and the threat of intimacy dissolved. The gaze of the woman is normally directed at the reader: this is actually one of the strictest conventions observed in the presentation of the image. The male who locks on to this gaze must by definition dominate it; the penis here again becomes the phallus, the imperial power which men are able to exert over women. Some pornographic magazines carry columns in which readers' sexual problems are discussed and responded to. But the bulk of the letters in such periodicals are utterly different from those collected by Stopes. In contrast to the problem-oriented letters, they are concerned to document prowess; again, they recount discrete sexual episodes.

In these episodes, one motif is pervasive. It is sexual pleasure, not in fact of the male but of the female, and usually presented in a very particular way. These are tales of women ecstatic in their sexuality, but always under the sway of the phallus. Women whimper, pant and quiver, but the men are silent, orchestrating the events which come to pass. The expressions of female delight are detailed with an attention far in excess of whatever is offered of the male experience itself. The rapture of the women is never in doubt; yet the point of the stories is not to understand or empathise with the sources and nature of female sexual pleasure, rather to tame and isolate it.[13] Events are described in terms of the reactions of the female, but in such a way as to make feminine desire just as episodic as that of the male. Men thus get to know what women want, and how to cope with female desire, on their own terms.

Pornography easily becomes addictive because of its sub-stitutive character. Women's complicity is ensured, but pornographic representation cannot hold in check the con-tradictory elements of male sexuality. The sexual pleasure which the female demonstrates comes with a price tag attached – for the creature who can give evidence of such frenzy can also be seen as imposing demands that have to be fulfilled. Failure is not openly displayed, but lurks as the unstated presumption of desire; rage, blame and awe of women are unmistakably mixed with the devotion these stories also betray. The normalising effects of soft pornog-raphy probably explain its mass appeal, rather than the fact that more explicit pornographic material may not be as readily available commercially. Hard pornography, in some of its many versions at least, might be more threatening, even though its explicitness may seem to cater most fully to the male 'quest'. Power here is no longer limited by the 'consent of the governed' – the complicit gaze of the woman – but appears as much more open, direct and forcibly imposed. For some, of course, that precisely is its attraction.

Yet hard pornography also operates at the outer borderline of phallic sexuality, disclosing the threatening freedoms of plastic sexuality on the other side.

Male sexual violence

Force and violence are part of all orders of domination. In the orthodox domain of politics, the question arises of how far power is hegemonic, such that violence is resorted to only when the legitimate order breaks down, or how far, alternatively, violence expresses the real nature of state power. A similar debate crops up in the literature concerned with pornography and sexual violence. Some have argued that the growth of hard pornography, particularly where violence is directly represented, depicts the inner truth of male sexuality as a whole.[14] It has further been suggested that violence against women, especially rape, is the main prop of men's control over them.[15] Rape shows the reality of the rule of the phallus.

It seems clear that there is a continuum, not a sharp break, between male violence towards women and other forms of intimidation and harassment. Rape, battering and even the murder of women often contain the same core elements as non-violent heterosexual encounters, the subduing and conquest of the sexual object.[16] Is pornography, then, the theory and rape the practice, as some have declared? In answering this question, it is important to determine if sexual violence is part of the long-standing male oppression of women, or whether it is related to the changes discussed in this book.

The impulse to subordinate and humiliate women, as the preceding discussion of masculine sexuality indicates, is probably a generic aspect of male psychology. Yet it is arguable (although certainly such a view is contentious) that male control of women in pre-modern cultures did not depend primarily upon the practice of violence against them. It was ensured above all through the 'rights of ownership' over women that men characteristically held, coupled to the principle of separate spheres. Women were ofter exposed to male violence, particularly within the domestic setting; equally important, however, they were protected from the public arenas within which men subjected one another to violence. This is why, in the premodern development of Europe, rape flourished 'mainly on the margins; at the frontiers, in colonies, in states at war and in states of nature; amongst marauding, invading armies'.[17]

The list is a formidable one, and horrifying enough in its own way. Yet violence in these circumstances was rarely directed specifically at women: at these 'margins' violence in general was pronounced and rape was one activity among other forms of brutality and slaughter, primarily involving men as destroyers and destroyed. Characteristic of such marginal situations was the fact that women were not as separated from male domains as was normally the case; nor could men ensure their safety.

In modern societies, things are very different. Women live and work in anonymous public settings far more often than they ever did before and the 'separate and unequal' divisions which insulated the sexes have substantially crumbled. It makes more sense in current times than it did previously to suppose that male sexual violence has become a basis of sexual control. In other words, a large amount of male sexual violence now stems from insecurity and inadequacy rather than from a seamless continuation of patriarchal dominance. Violence is a destructive reaction to the waning of female complicity.

Save in conditions of war, men are perhaps today more violent towards women than they are towards one another. There are many types of male sexual violence against women, but at least some have the consequence noted before: they keep sexuality episodic. This might be the principal – although certainly not the only – trait which links such violence to pornography. If such is the case, it follows that pornographic literature, or a good deal of it, is part of the hegemonic system of domination, with sexual violence being a secondary support rather than an exemplar of phallic power.

Of course, it would be absurd to claim that there is a unitary norm of masculinity, and it would be false to suppose that all men are reluctant to embrace change. Moreover, sexual violence is not confined to the activities of men. Women are quite often physically violent towards men in domestic settings; violence seems a not uncommon feature of lesbian relationships, at least in some contexts. Studies of female sexual violence in the US describe cases of lesbian rape, physical battering and assault with guns, knives and other lethal weapons.[18] Most of the men who wrote to Marie Stopes were concerned to solve their sexual problems in order to increase the satisfaction of their female partners. Many men who regularly visit prostitutes wish to assume a passive, not an active role, whether or not this involves actual masochistic practices. Some gay men find their greatest pleasure in being submissive, but many are also able to switch roles. They have been more successful than most heterosexuals in isolating differential power and confining it to the arena of sexuality as such. 'There are fantasies', as one gay man expresses it, 'that trap us and fantasies that free us . . . Sexual fantasies, when consciously employed, can create a counter-order, a kind of subversion, and a little space into which we can escape, especially when they scramble all those neat and oppressive distinctions between active and passive, masculine and feminine, dominant and submissive.'[19]

Female sexuality: the problem of complementarity

If we accepted the principle that each sex is what the other is not, there would be a simple meshing between male and female sexuality. Things are not so clear-cut, because all children share similarities in psychosexual evolution, particularly in the early part of their lives. Whatever the limitations of his ideas when viewed from the perspective of today, Freud was the first to make this apparent. Little girls have a similar erotic history to boys – although for Freud the reason is that their early sexuality, as he put it, 'is of a wholly masculine character'.[20] Difference intrudes when both sexes realise that the little girl has something missing; each thinks she has been castrated.

In Freud's view, psychologically speaking there is only one genital organ, that of the male. Although the genitals of the girl are at first a matter of indifference to the boy – until the threat of castration is fantasised – she quickly sees what she lacks is a penis, and wants to have it. Even at the stage of the Oedipus complex the experience of the girl is not directly complementary to that of the boy. For, as Freud puts it, 'it is only in male children that there occurs a fateful simultaneous conjunction of love for one parent and hatred of the other as a rival'.[21] The girl turns away from the mother, and blames her for her lack of a penis, although she cannot in the same way identify with the father or displace her aggression on to him.

In their 'reversal' of Freud, Chodorow and authors writing from a similar viewpoint introduce greater complementarity than was presumed in the original Freudian account. According to them, the girl preserves those features of psychosexual development which the boy has forgone; the boy develops traits, an instrumental attitude towards the world and so forth, which the girl does not possess, or which are only weakly elaborated. From the beginning, the mother's relation to a boy is different from that she takes towards a girl. She treats him as more of a distinct being than the girl, who is loved in a more 'narcissistic' fashion.[22] Each sex gains, and each loses, although boys lose more. Girls have a stronger sense of gender identity, but a weaker sense of their autonomy and individuality; boys are more capable of independent action, although the emotional price to be paid for this capacity is high.

Pursuing the themes introduced earlier, let me modify and historicise this interpretation, and try to show why an undue emphasis upon complementarity should be avoided. The invention of motherhood creates a situation in which, in the eyes of both the little girl and little boy, the mother is perceived as more all-powerful, as well as all-loving, than was the case in earlier generations. That power and love, however, are also associated with greater respect for the autonomy of the child, even very early on in life, than was previously typical (although there are many empirical instances in which such respect is largely withheld).

The break with the mother on the part of the boy has the consequence that his dependence upon women becomes masked and, on an unconscious and often on a conscious level, denied; it is difficult in later life to integrate sexuality into a reflexive narrative of self. What men tend to repress, to repeat, is not the capability to love, but the emotional autonomy important for the sustaining of intimacy. Girls have a greater chance of achieving such autonomy, which depends more upon communication rather than the propensity to express emotions as such. Communicative resourcefulness of this sort should be regarded as a matter of competence just as much as that 'instrumental competence' which males are prone to develop.

The reliance of men upon women for doing the work of intimacy is expressed, not only in the domain of sexuality, but in friendship also. There are organisations, like clubs or sports teams, which, because of their all-male character, provide situations in which male fraternity can be developed and consolidated. Yet fraternity – bonds that come from shared, and exclusive, male experience – is not the same as friendship, considered from the point of view of the characteristics of the pure relationship. An in-depth study of two hundred men and women in the US showed that two-thirds of the men interviewed could not name a close friend. Of those who could, the friend was most likely to be a woman. Three-quarters of the women in the research could easily mention one or more close friends, and for them it was virtually always a woman. Married as well as single women named other women as their best friends.[23]

For girls and boys it is a shock to acknowledge the power of the phallus – for the very competence they have developed is threatened, if not even completely overturned by this discovery. In the case of the boy, in the area of sexuality, the phallus becomes a signifier of an ambivalent capacity to dominate women. The more the phallus becomes the penis, however, the more it has to be 'tested out' in episodic encounters which combine risk and pleasure. Rather than complementarity, the situation here is one of mutual dislocation and involves contradictory elements in the case of girls as well as boys. The frustration of the girl's wish to be like the father is acute, although it does not necessarily compartmentalise the personality in the manner characteristic of boys. It can be seen why despair at men, alternating with an idealising of them, should become so mixed up in the mind of the girl. The father symbolises separation and 'acting on' the world; yet he is also unattainable. The capacity of the girl to love becomes fused with an overwhelming desire to be loved and cared for.

Is there any sense in which submissiveness is a peculiar feature of feminine psychosexual development, as the stereotype might have it? I do not think that there is. For boys and girls alike impulses towards submissiveness and mastery become interconnected, and the wish to be dominated is a powerful residue of the repressed awareness of the mother's early influence. Both sexes develop the capacity for caring, although this characteristically takes divergent forms. Unless a boy becomes completely alienated psychologically from his mother during or after infancy, he retains the capability and desire to care for the other; but such caring normally takes on an 'instrumental' character. Nurturance, in the sense of emotional support, corresponds much more to the capabilities developed by the little girl. Even here, however, it would be a mistake to suppose that the abilities of the one sex merely complement those of the other, for each develops in contradiction.

The 'absent father', the father who has only a shadowy existence during the early period of the upbringing of the child, has a particular significance for the little girl. He can be idealised because of his remoteness, but he also appears as dangerous – this air of menace often becomes part of his very attractiveness. Being less at the centre of the child's life than the mother, he is also less susceptible to her communicative skills. He must be 'converted', won over, yet he is also distant and, as it seems on the level of the unconscious, unattainable. His refractory qualities must be brought under control if autonomy is to be achieved; the paradox is that if he were fully to be won over, the little girl would know that something had gone wrong; for he wins her respect not as the sexual possessor of the mother, but because of the very maintenance of his 'separateness'.

Anger, as well as the desire for love, fuels the episodic sexuality of men; quite often, it is the basis of masochism and the desire to submit, a syndrome connected to shame. Anger and shame, however, also form characteristics of the upbringing of women. The little girl loves her mother, but resents her as well: in distancing herself from her, via identification with the father, she transfers her resentment to him. Idealised though he might be, he cannot make up for what she has to sacrifice in seeking to win him over. His very remoteness, compared with the proximity to her mother the child has enjoyed, further promotes such ambivalence. Men cannot be trusted; they will always let you down.

To understand more fully the relation between shame and psychosexual development, we can go back to Freud's interpretation of feminity, where it is linked closely with narcissism. According to Freud, women have a narcissistic investment in their bodies which men largely lack, a result of the girl's reaction to the fact of her 'castration'. The little girl abandons masturbation and gives up interest in the clitoris, which is so manifestly inadequate. Her eroticism becomes diffuse, rather than concentrated upon a prime pleasure-giving organ. She sees herself only in the reflection of male desire. Hence the woman's need does not, in Freud's words, 'lie in the direction of loving' but more in that of 'being loved'; 'the man who fulfils this condition is the one who finds favour' with her.[24] Women need not just to be admired, but told that they are appreciated and valued. Deprived of narcissistic confirmation in their early lives, women thereafter only find security in the mirror of love provided by the adoring other. Needless to say, men are as ill-equipped to meet this requirement as they are to respond to female eroticism. Hence the oft-heard complaint of women that their male partners are clumsy, have no real understanding of what brings them satisfaction and so on.[25]

The conclusions Freud draws are surely in some part correct, but not the arguments deployed to reach them. Two separate issues are raised by these arguments: female sexuality and the eroticising of the body, on the one hand, and the wish for reassurance about being loved on the other. We may suppose that both sexes, in fact, once the break with the mother is made, need reassurance that they are still loved. The need of the boy for love, however, contrary to Freud's view, is greater or more urgent than that of the girl, largely because it tends to be more deeply buried. The boy's reassurance comes from the rule of the phallus (the assertion of social status and power) and, in the area of sexual behaviour itself, from episodic sexuality. Such sexuality denies the very emotional dependence that fuels it.

Freud's interpretation of female sexuality made a lasting impression upon the later psychoanalytic literature. Women's sexuality was seen as essentially passive, a view which reinforced the current stereotypes. In the light of current changes in sexual behaviour, it has become apparent that, to the degree that such a portrayal corresponded to reality, it was the result of social constraints placed upon women rather than enduring psychosexual characteristics. The image of the sexually voracious woman, of course, has long existed alongside that of female passivity; Freud's account emphasised one picture at the expense of the other.

The diffuse eroticism of which Freud spoke should properly be regarded as potentially subversive rather than a negative reaction to a situation of 'loss'. The clitoris is not the functional equivalent of the penis, nor is female sexual pleasure defined by a failure to match up to the standard set by the male. It can be presumed that both sexes, as infants, retain the capacity to eroticise the body. The boy tends to give this up in favour of a more genitally focused regime, as part of the Oedipal transition. Girls, on the other hand, are more able to sustain it, and therefore also more able to integrate specifically genital sensations with other experiences and attachments – in fact, they are liable to find sexual activity shorn of these wider connections unrewarding.[26]

Gender, intimacy and care

Let me sum up the implications of the preceding discussion. While it is possible, as Freud believed, and even very likely, that there are more or less universal features of sexual psychology, I put that question largely to one side. A distinctive feature of socialisation in the recent period, characteristic of most strata in modern societies, has been the prominent role of the mother in early child care. Mother–infant relations are influenced by the 'invention of motherhood' as well as reflecting other changes which distinguish modern from pre-modern institutions. The dominance of the mother has profound psychological consequences for both sexes, and is at the origin of some of the most pervasive aspects of gender difference today.

Men have problems with intimacy: this assertion we hear again and again in the therapeutic literature as well as elsewhere. But what does it mean? If the analysis I have suggested is valid, we cannot simply say that women tend to be more capable of developing emotional sympathy with others than are most men. Nor, to repeat a banality, can we accept that women are in touch with their feelings in a way that men typically are not. Intimacy is above all a matter of emotional communication, with others and with the self, in a context of interpersonal equality. Women have prepared the way for an expansion of the domain of intimacy in their role as the emotional revolutionaries of modernity. Certain psychological dispositions have been the condition and outcome of this process, as have also the material changes which have allowed women to stake a claim to equality. On the psychological level, male difficulties with intimacy are above all the result of two things: a schismatic view of women that can be traced to an unconscious reverence for the mother, and a lapsed emotional narrative of self. In social circumstances in which women are no longer complicit with the role of the phallus, the traumatic elements of maleness are thus exposed more plainly to view.

All psychodynamic mechanisms, in the individual case, are complex and there is not a straightforward complementarity between male and femal psychology. Thus a generalisation about either 'men' or 'women' as a whole, even leaving aside the diversity of pre-modern or non-modern cultures, has to be qualified. As in other parts of this book, whenever I speak of 'women' or 'men' without qualification, there is always an implicit parenthesis which adds 'in many instances'. Episodic sexuality, for example, as was stressed previously, is not confined to men; it is a mechanism of power, and its defensive attributes have some usefulness for women also. The idea that 'men can't love' is plainly false, and should not – again for reasons mentioned before – be equated directly with men's difficulties with intimacy. Much male sexuality is energised by a frustrated search for love, which, however, is feared as well as desired. Many men are not capable of loving others as equals, in circumstances of intimacy, but they are well able to offer love and care to those inferior in power (women, children) or with whom they share an unstated rapport (buddies, members of a fraternity).

Nor are difficulties with intimacy confined to men. Women's relation to male power is ambivalent. The demand for equality may jostle psychologically with the search for a male figure who is emotionally remote and authoritative. The development of respect based upon the equal and independent capabilities of the other thus poses problems for both sexes, something which no doubt seeps over into homosexual relationships too. The communication of feelings, moreover, is not in and of itself enough for intimacy. In so far as such communication is bound up with narcissism, it is a bid for power rather than providing for the development of confluent love.

Masculinity as loss: is this theme consistent with the reality of the persistence of patriarchal domination? For the sexual division of labour remains substantially intact; at home and at work, in most contexts of modern societies, men are largely unwilling to release their grip upon the reins of power. Power is harnessed to interests and obviously there are sheerly material considerations which help explain why this is so. However, in so far as male power is based on the compliance of women, and the economic and emotional services which women provide, it is under threat.

NOTES

1 Andy Metcalf: Introduction to Andy Metcalf and Martin Humphries: *The Sexuality of Men*, London: Pluto, 1985, p. 1.
2 For the best recent discussion, see Teresa Brennan: *Between Feminism and Psychoanalysis*, London: Routledge, 1989.
3 Anthony Giddens: 'Structuralism, post-structuralism and the production of culture', in Anthony Giddens and Jonathan Turner: *Social Theory Today*, Cambridge: Polity, 1987.
4 Nancy Chodorow: *The Reproduction of Mothering*, Berkeley: University of California Press, 1978.
5 Janine Chasseguet-Smirgel: 'Freud and female sexuality', *International Journal of Psychoanalysis*, vol. 57, 1976.
6 Jessica Benjamin: *The Bonds of Love*, London: Virago, 1990.
7 Hans Leowald: 'Waning of the Oedipus complex', in *Papers on Psychoanalysis*, New Haven: Yale University Press, 1983.
8 Heather Formani: *Men. The Darker Continent*, London: Mandarin, 1991, p. 13.
9 Cf. Michael Ross: *The Married Homosexual Man*, London: Routledge, 1983.
10 Lesley A. Hall: *Hidden Anxieties. Male Sexuality, 1900–1950*, Cambridge: Polity, 1991.
11 Ibid., p. 121.
12 Andy Moye: 'Pornography', in Metcalf and Humphries, *The Sexuality of Men*.
13 Ibid., pp. 68–9.
14 Andrea Dworkin: *Pornography: Men Possessing Women*, London: Women's Press, 1981.
15 Susan Griffin: 'Rape, the all-American crime', *Ramparts*, vol. 10, 1973; Susan Brownmiller: *Against Our Will*, London: Penguin, 1977.
16 Liz Kelly: *Surviving Sexual Violence*, Cambridge: Polity, 1988.

17 Roy Porter: 'Does rape have an historical meaning?', in Sylvana Tomaselli and Roy Porter: *Rape*, Oxford: Blackwell, 1986, p. 235.

18 Karay Lobel: *Naming the Violence*, Seattle: Seal, 1986.

19 Quoted in Lynne Segal: *Slow Motion*, London: Virago, 1990, p. 262.

20 Sigmund Freud: *Three Essays on the Theory of Sexuality, Standard Edition*, London: Hogarth, 1953.

21 Ibid.

22 George Stambolian: *Male Fantasies/Gay Realities*, New York: Sea Horse, 1984, pp. 159–60.

23 Lillian Rubin: *Intimate Strangers*, New York: Harper and Row, 1983. See also Stuart Miller: *Men and Friendship*, London: Gateway, 1983.

24 Sigmund Freud: 'On narcissism', *Standard Edition*, vol. 14, p. 89.

25 Janine Chasseguet-Smirgel: *Female Sexuality*, Ann Arbor: University of Michigan Press, 1970, pp. 76–83.

26 Shere Hite: *Women and Love*, London: Viking, 1988.

8

CONTRADICTIONS OF THE PURE RELATIONSHIP

Especially in so far as they are primarily or partly located in the unconscious, the psychological traits discussed in the previous chapter set up fundamental tensions within the emergent world of pure relationships. To trace these out, I shall concentrate upon aspects of the pure relationship in same-sex encounters – specifically, those of lesbian women. The strategy might seem an odd one, following on from an interpretation of the psychic characteristics of male and female sexuality. But to see how far the psychological divisions which tend to separate men and women might prove destructive of the pure relationship, it is worth considering its intrinsic dynamics – and in some ways these are most easily studied when the heterosexual element is taken out.

Without worrying too much about how representative the material is, I shall draw heavily upon certain sections of those marvellously reflexive documents, the Hite reports. The Hite surveys set out to 'chart an ideological revolution in progress', but they also convey the awareness that the documents analysed contribute directly to that process. Hite's first long 'essay questionnaire' was distributed in 1972–6, and her subsequent first volume based upon responses from 3,500 women in the US. A notable feature of that study and the succeeding volumes was their emphasis that sexuality should be not only studied through the musings of 'experts' – Kinsey, Masters and Johnson and the rest – but approached through the accounts given by ordinary people. The purpose of the project, in Hite's words, was 'to let *women* define their own sexuality', to allow them 'to speak out about how they feel about sex, how they define their own sexuality, and what sexuality means to them'.

Hite found that 11 per cent of the women in her study (volume 3) had sexual relationships only with other women; a further 7 per cent did so on occasion. No particular statistical significance can be attached to these figures, but it is worth noting that a substantial proportion of her respondents who were above the age of forty were involved in sexual relationships with women for the first time in their lives. Virtually all of these had previously been in heterosexual marriages. Over 80 per cent of the lesbian women, at the time of the study, were in relationships of some duration.

Most lesbian women may be in long-term relationships, but they have difficulty in gaining a sense of security in them. One woman comments:

A non-conventional relationship, with no rules, is difficult. In a marriage, in the traditional sense, if just by chance the roles that people are taught happen to fit two individuals, then that's a pretty good arrangement . . . But for most of us in gay relationships . . . there aren't any rules, really, so you're kind of making up your own as you go along. It's this constant thing of trying to figure out how it works.

Yet since marriage 'in the traditional sense' is disappearing, it is the gays who are the pioneers in this respect – the prime everyday experimenters. They have for some while experienced what is becoming more and more commonplace for heterosexual couples.

The pure relationship: breaking and making

In heterosexual marriage in earlier periods past sexual encounters were normally 'written out' by both partners as of little significance for the future. Women usually came to marriage with their 'virtue' intact, while the philandering of men was consigned to the category of an acceptable episodic sexuality. A relationship today, however, has to be set apart both from what went before and also from the other involvements, sexual or otherwise, which the individuals might have. A person with whom a partner was in a previous relationship might live on in the minds of one or both; even if prior emotional ties have become quite thoroughly broken, a current relationship is likely to be permeated by their residues. If it be recognised that all adult personal attachments recall aspects of infantile experience, so also do experiences of loss; and in the domain of pure relationships individuals must often now cope with multiple passages of this sort.

Breaking up is an ordeal for gay women because of the negotiated status of their relationships and the particularly 'open' character of homosexual self-identity. 'When we broke up I was really confused. I wondered if I was really a lesbian or if she was the only woman I could love.' This is a woman describing the dissolution of her first sexual relationship with another woman. She adds, 'for many of my lesbian friends, it was the same, the first breakup was devastating because it opened up everything for questioning again'. She has also suffered at the termination of other relationships that had lasted several years or more. One person speaks for most when she says:

> Sometimes I get tired of going through life negotiating relationships and working it out. Like, will I ever arrive at some kind of plateau where I finally get the results of my

labours? Once you've run the last mile, they may still leave you for a younger, or more intelligent, or older, or whatever woman – or a man!

There is a structural contradiction in the pure relationship, centring upon commitment, which many of Hite's respondents acknowledge. To generate commitment and develop a shared history, an individual must give of herself to the other. That is, she must provide, in word and deed, some kind of guarantees to the other that the relationship can be sustained for an indefinite period. Yet a present-day relationship is not, as marriage once was, a 'natural condition' whose durability can be taken for granted short of certain extreme circumstances. It is a feature of the pure relationship that it can be terminated, more or less at will, by either partner at any particular point. For a relationship to stand a chance of lasting, commitment is necessary; yet anyone who commits herself without reservations risks great hurt in the future, should the relationship become dissolved.

Some three-quarters of Hite's sample dwell upon their insecurities in respect of love. 'I am always questioning whether she really loves me, or if I love her more'; 'Sometimes I feel love, other times ignored. Am I satisfied? No'; 'I feel more needy than I think she does. I feel loved, but I am somewhat insecure. I want her to want me more. Yet, I would dislike it greatly if she depended too much on me or drained me.' However, most find sexual relationships with other women more intimate and equal than those with men. A general awareness that new models of love should be developed, and that gay relationships provide a context in which this can be achieved, is apparent. 'In love', as one woman puts it, 'is explosive, obsessive, irrational, wonderful, heady, dreamy. Loving is long work, trust, communication, commitment, pain, pleasure.'

The conflict between sexual excitement, which is often

short-lived, and more durable forms of caring for the other emerges strongly. Yet many also observe that the intensity of their sexual responsiveness and satisfaction depends upon the degree of closeness they feel to the other. Over 80 per cent say they are able to talk easily and intimately with their partners. 'She is respectfully attentive, she pays attention to me when I need it, and I do to her. I'm more likely to state my desires, but I encourage her to do what she wants and say whatever she feels.'[1] Economic inequalities are less marked than in most heterosexual relationships; and sharing domestic tasks, even if this frequently produces clashes, seems to be more or less universal.

In the pure relationship, trust has no external supports, and has to be developed on the basis of intimacy. Trust is a vesting of confidence in the other and also in the capability of the mutual bond to withstand future traumas. This is more than a matter of good faith only, problematic as that may be in itself. To trust the other is also to gamble upon the capability of the individual actually to be able to act with integrity. The tendency of sexual relationships to be dyadic (not to be confused with monogamous) is probably to some degree a result of the unconscious desire to recapitulate that feeling of exclusivity which the infant enjoys with its mother. The 'specialness' which one finds in another is, as Freud says, a 'refinding' in this sense. Yet the dyadic character of sexual relationships also tends to be enforced by the nature of the trust presumed. For trust, when we speak of trust in persons, is not a quality capable of indefinite expansion.

The shared history which two individuals develop together at some points inevitably closes off others, who become part of the generalised 'outside'. Exclusiveness is not a guarantee of trust, but it is nevertheless an important stimulus to it. Intimacy means the disclosure of emotions and actions which the individual is unlikely to hold up to a wider public gaze. Indeed, the disclosure of what is kept from other people is one of the main psychological markers likely to call forth trust from the other and to be sought after in return. It is easy to see how the self-disclosure which intimacy presumes can produce codependence if it does not go along with the preservation of autonomy. If the psychological 'giving' to the other is not mutual, and reasonably well balanced, one individual is likely to define her or his needs without regard to the other, expecting her or him to go along with them.

Of course, a partner in a relationship might make sure that she or he has a circle of friends, as well as others who can be relied upon in times of difficulty. Yet since trust cannot be expanded indefinitely, there are priorities in such decisions. Just like lovers, friends normally require markers of intimacy, information that is special to them alone. Someone who confides more about her feelings and experiences to a friend than to her lover is likely to have reservations about her relationship with that lover. For many heterosexual couples this problem is in a certain sense 'solved' by the very fact that women so often find their male partners difficult to 'talk to'. They are able to put up markers of intimacy with their women friends which a husband or male lover may repudiate.

Giving certain conditions, the pure relationship can provide a facilitating social environment for the reflexive project of self. Boundaries, personal space and the rest, as the therapeutic manuals say, are needed for individuals to flourish in a relationship rather than slide into codependence. Yet it is plain that there are also large areas of possible tension and conflict here. The shared history that a relationship develops can serve to screen off troubles in the outside world; one or both individuals may become dependent, not so much upon the other, but upon the relationship and its routines in a fixated way, as a means of insulating themselves from a full engagement with other social tasks or obligations. Achieving a balance between autonomy and dependence is problematic.

The mobile nature of self-identity does not necessarily sit easily with the demands of pure relationships. Trust must somehow accommodate itself to the different trajectories of development that partners might follow. There always has to be a certain licence in trust. To trust someone means forgoing opportunities to keep tabs on them or force their activities within some particular mould. Yet the autonomy that is granted to the other will not necessarily be used in such a way as to fulfil the needs that the partner has in the relationship. People 'grow apart' – this is a common enough observation. Yet more subtle influences can be involved. A shift in the narrative of self, for instance, however it might be brought about, typically affects the distribution of power in a relationship, and can nudge it in the direction of codependence.

Lesbianism and male sexuality

Each sex is a dark continent to the other, and the discussion offered in the previous chapter indicates readily enough why this tends to be so. A clear sense of relief at escaping from the sexual attentions of men pervades the attitudes of many of Hite's respondents, even among those who continue to engage in heterosexual encounters. Hite's findings echo those of Charlotte Wolff and others, that bisexual women usually have much stronger attachments to other women than they do to men, even when they are in heterosexual marriages.[2]

Plastic sexuality, if fully developed, would imply a neutral attitude towards the penis. Few women in Hite's study, or that of Wolff, are able or inclined to move freely between women and men, however much they mix up their sexual experiences. Yet lesbian women do break the stereotype that women are naturally monogamous. Most of Hite's respondents regard monogamy as a desirable ideal, if they are in a reasonably long-term relationship. But this has more to do with a recognition of the centrality of trust than with an aversion to sexual experimentation as such. Many women speak of the difficulties either they or their partners have with remaining monogamous, at least after an initial period of intense physical attraction to the partner has faded.

The episodic sexuality of men seems clearly related to an unconscious endeavour to reclaim and subdue the all-powerful mother. That kind of extreme sexual adventurism seems largely absent among women. Yet we know that the desire to subdue is not limited to male psychology, and it is not surprising to find that some women use promiscuity as a means of tempering the commitment which a primary relationship presupposes. 'She's a horrible philanderer', one woman remarks of her lover

and always has been. I put up with it for three years. We lived together two years. I finally . . . moved out. I still see her and sleep with her, but I sleep with other women too. After all that time of watching her go out with others, I decided to try it too – now I like it and I'm not sure I'm basically monogamous any more either.

A smaller proportion of lesbian than heterosexual married women have had, or are having, affairs outside their primary relationships, but the numbers are still substantial (about a third among Hite's respondents). 'I have had sex outside of my relationships, every one'; 'I love women. I love to flirt. I love the seduction'; 'I was not in love; I was in lust' – wouldn't one think this was heterosexual men, rather than lesbian women, speaking?

However, there are differences. Most heterosexual

women keep their affairs hidden from their partners, but among homosexuals non-monogamous sex is typically either carried on with the knowledge and acquiescence of the partner or very quickly comes to the other's awareness. The reason seems to be the higher level of communication found in woman-to-woman as opposed to heterosexual relationships. Departures from monogamy are more often openly discussed and monogamy is less of a residue of traditional norms of marriage than a standard established in a consensual way. Where other liaisons are not brought out into the open from the beginning, they tend to come to light at some point or another.

A few women seem to miss the episodic sex that encounters with men make possible, but which is rarer in sexual involvements with other women. One continues to have sex with men specifically for that purpose. Another says, 'I find it almost impossible to have the kind of "fun" in essentially impersonal sexual encounters with women that I used to have with men. There is no way that you don't get to know the other women in the process – there is a lot more talking, more affection – you become friends, at the very least.' According to Hite's figures, over 60 per cent of lesbian women remain close and long-term friends with their ex-lovers after the breakup of a relationship.[3]

A prominent feature of the reportage of the lesbian women concerns the intense and sought-after nature of sexual pleasure. Women want sex? Certainly these women do, and are active in the pursuit of sexual satisfaction, both inside and outside relationships. If sexual pleasure be measured by orgasmic response – a dubious index, as many have said, but surely not devoid of value when placed against the sexual deprivations suffered by women in the past – lesbian sex appears more successful than heterosexual activity. Moreover, there is greater equality in the giving and taking of sexual experience: 'There's a bond between us that my experience with men could never compare to'; 'I like women's ways, bodies, passions, gentleness/power'; 'I have never felt pressured to have sex by a woman. I was *always* pressured by men.' For the most part these emphases seem compatible with, and actively serve to produce, sexual responsiveness. These women give the lie to the idea that the eroticising of the female body is achieved at the expense of genital sensation. The two in fact go together, something that is entirely compatible with the influence of plastic sexuality.

In gay relationships, male as well as female, sexuality can be witnessed in its complete separation from reproduction. The sexuality of gay women is organised of necessity almost wholly with regard to the perceived implications of the pure relationship. That is to say, the plasticity of sexual response is channelled above all by a recognition of the tastes of the partners and their view about what is or is not enjoyable and tolerable. Differential power may by reimported through a proclivity, for example, for sado-masochistic sex. One woman says:

> I like rough, passionate sex because it goes beyond the barriers of 'niceness' that so many women build around themselves. There's no feeling of holding back, as there so often is with politically correct gentle sex – 'S and L', as one of my friends has dubbed it (sweetness and light that is). My current lover and I have experimented some with S/M and bondage and found it very exciting and sexy. Everything we've done has been totally consensual and the 'bottom' (who it is varies) always has control, along with the illusion of being out of control. We've included things like spanking, whipping, hair pulling, and biting, never to the point of injury or even marking. What makes it so good is the feeling of completely letting go.[4]

One might see here the return of the phallus and in a somewhat obnoxious form. To some extent this may be correct, but a different interpretation could also be proposed. In lesbian relationships (as among male gays also), attitudes and traits, 'prohibited' in the pure relationship can potentially be acted upon, including instrumental control and the exercise of formal power. Confined within the sphere of sexuality and turned into fantasy – rather than, as has always been usual, determined from the outside – dominance perhaps helps to neutralise aggression which would otherwise make itself felt elsewhere.

As in other respects, what might appear to be a retrograde characteristic of woman-to-woman sexual relationships could actually provide a model for ethically defensible heterosexual activity. Consensual sado-masochism need not be offered as a recipe for rewarding sexual experience, but the principle it expresses is capable of generalisation. Plastic sexuality might become a sphere which no longer contains the detritus of external compulsions, but instead takes its place as one among other forms of self-exploration and moral construction. Perhaps here one could read a quite different meaning into the writings of de Sade from those ordinarily suggested. In de Sade, power, pain and death come to invest themselves wholly in sex, and are played out through perversion. The phallus rules everything and sexuality is drained of any vestiges of tenderness – or so it seems. Yet de Sade separates female sexuality wholly from reproduction and celebrates its chronic escape from subordination to phallic concerns. His representation of sex, which concentrates everything else within it, could be seen as an ironic metaphorical device, indicating the innocence of sexuality itself.

Homosexuality and the episodic encounter

Episodic sexuality is most developed among women in the culture of some types of lesbian clubs and bars. Bar life is sometimes concentrated upon cruising, the search for transient sexual partners. A newcomer to the bar culture comments that, for a long while, 'I just couldn't understand why I kept lucking out in the bars.' Her education and background, she continues, didn't seem to impress anyone. Then it dawned on her that the main things that counted in forming liaisons were looks and 'on the spot attractiveness'. 'It was that simple . . . No one in the bar was interested in meeting someone she could take home to meet Mother.'[5]

Short-term, depersonalised liaisons: these are by no means absent from lesbian relationships. Given that many gay men establish long-term sexual ties with one another, one should not exaggerate the contrasts between female and male homosexuality. Yet episodic sexuality among some gay men is intensified well beyond anything found in lesbian communities. When the bath-houses existed, for example, many men who attended sought out multiple sexual experiences each evening; most would be disappointed if they only had one sexual encounter during the course of several hours. In his study of the bath-house culture in the 1960s, for example, Martin Hoffman interviewed one young man who, as the passive receptor, often had some fifty sexual contacts in the course of an evening.[6]

Bath-house sex, as is true of various other contexts of male gay sexual activity, was generally anonymous. The men who went there usually had no social contact with each other save for the most casual of conversations. They had no knowledge of the nature of each other's lives in the outside world and addressed one another only by first names. A new meaning here is given to transience; compared with such encounters, the anonymous heterosexual episode portrayed in Last Tango in Paris seems like a deep and enduring involvement.

The man referred to by Hoffman had been married and was the father of two children. Male bisexuality is so characteristic of the sexual behaviour of men today that it is as 'orthodox' a form of sexual orientation as heterosexuality. The proportion of 'heterosexual' men who engage regularly in episodic homosexual activity has increased markedly over the recent period – in spite of the impact of AIDS. Researchers have estimated that, in the US, 40 per cent of married men at some point during their married lives engage in regular sex with other men; others have claimed the proportion to be even higher.[7]

The defensive aspects of episodic sexuality in this guise seem clear enough. It can be seen as a wholesale male flight from the connections which link sexuality, self-identity and intimacy. Where women are no longer complicit, episodic homosexuality is a collusive effort of men to resist the implications of gender equality. Commitment to the rights of the other in the marital relationship is kept at bay emotionally through the distancing effect of episodic encounters.

Can the same be said of men who are more explicitly gay and repudiate all sexual contacts with women? Given that resentment towards women is part of male psychology on a very general level, gay men in some sense cope with ambivalence by detaching themselves from it altogether. Yet it would be wrong to see an orientation towards episodic sexuality only in negative terms. Like lesbians, male gays place in question the traditional heterosexual integration of marriage and monogamy. As understood in institutionalised marriage, monogamy was always tied to the double standard and therefore to patriarchy. It was a normative demand upon men, but for many honoured only in the breach. In a world of plastic sexuality and pure relationships, however, monogamy has to be 'reworked' in the context of commitment and trust. Monogamy refers, not to the relationship itself, but to sexual exclusiveness as a criterion of trust; 'fidelity' has no meaning except as an aspect of that integrity which trust in the other presumes.

Where episodic encounters do not form a control device

– or an addiction, as surely is the case in the instance described by Hoffman – they are in effect explorations of the possibilities offered by plastic sexuality. From this perspective, even in the shape of impersonal, fleeting contacts, episodic sexuality may be a positive form of everyday experiment. It reveals plastic sexuality for what it (implicitly) is: sex detached from its age-old subservience to differential power. Episodic gay sexuality of the bathhouse culture type thus expresses an equality which is absent from most heterosexual involvements, including transient ones. By its very nature, it permits power only in the form of sexual practice itself: sexual taste is the sole determinant. This is surely part of the pleasure and fulfilment that episodic sexuality can provide, when shorn of its compulsive characteristics.

The macho gay, the leather queen, the denim groupie – these are more than just ironic rejoinders to heterosexual masculinity. They are a visible deconstruction of maleness, and at the same time they affirm what taken for granted phallic power denies: that, in modern social life, self-identity, including sexual identity, is a reflexive achievement. In a parallel way, impersonal episodic sex is a critical commentary upon the subversion of sexual pleasure by its involvement with 'extrinsic' domination. It is likely to be defensive and compulsive to the degree to which it is driven by influences outside itself. Its intrinsic equality can only be fully redeemed if nourished through equalising influences in other milieux of social life. Episodic sexuality may usually be a way of avoiding intimacy, but it also offers a means of furthering or elaborating upon it. For sexual exclusiveness is only one way in which commitment to another is protected and integrity achieved. Central though it is to the rule of the phallus, it is not at all clear that episodic sexuality is inherently incompatible with emergent norms of the pure relationship.

Men and women: together or apart?

'I've been gay for thirty years. I've had long relationships, so have my friends, but almost nobody stays together "for life". We used to worry about this – we thought heterosexuals seemed to stay together far more than gay couples did.' The woman making this observation in Hite's study goes on to add: things have changed now. And so they have. The gay relationships described in Hite's investigations are frequently difficult, beset with problems and short-lived. In comparison with them, however, heterosexual relationships quite often seem like a battleground, where aggression and open fighting intermingle with a profound disaffection between the sexes. Hite found that almost her entire sample of heterosexual women respondents said that they want 'more verbal closeness' with their husbands; most report meeting resistance, or emotional disengagement, when they try to initiate closer communication. Women feel desperate about the continued infidelities of their partners, although a comparable proportion of them also engage in extramarital liaisons. They find emotional aridity in situations in which they expected continuing love. Hite puts things in the following way:

> Many women know they are not getting equal emotional support, esteem or respect in their relationships. And yet it can be difficult to describe definitively to a man just how he is projecting diminishing attitudes. Some of the ways this happens are so subtle in their expression that, while a woman may wind up feeling frustrated and on the defensive, she can find it almost impossible to say just why: pointing to the subtle thing said or done would look petty, like overreacting. But taken all together, it is no surprise when even one of these incidents can set off a major fight – or, more typically, another round of alienation which never gets resolved. These little incidents cut away at the relationship, making women

angry and finally causing love to dwindle down to a mere modest toleration.[8]

Equalisation is an intrinsic element in the transformation of intimacy, as is the possibility of communication. Men's anger against women today in some substantial part is a reaction against women's self-assertion, in the home, the workplace and elsewhere. Women are angry at men in turn because of the subtle and not so subtle ways in which men deny them material privileges claimed for themselves. Economic poverty for women, emotional poverty for men: is this the state of play in the relation between the sexes? The self-appointed advocates of men and women on both sides would say so, although each is likely to accuse the other of not fully acknowledging the sufferings of the other sex.

Picking up on the theme of masculinity as psychic damage, Herb Goldberg describes the 'hazards of being male' and speaks of masculine privilege as a myth.[9] Goldberg is a sensitive observer of the changes that have affected gender and sexuality, and sympathetic to the aims of the women's movement. In his writings, however, the complaints of women about men made in Hite's studies and echoed in myriad therapeutic manuals – that men are emotionally stunted, out of touch with their feelings and so forth – are seen as unhappy burdens men have to shoulder.

Here addiction once more appears in a central role. Many men, Goldberg says, have become 'zombies', driven by motives they barely understand. Modern culture is saturated by 'businessmen zombies, golf zombies, sports car zombies, playboy zombies': all are 'playing by the rules of the male game plan' and as a consequence 'have lost touch with, or are running away from, their feelings and awareness of themselves as people'. Women have protested against, and broken free from, their confinement to a domestic milieu and the limitations of self-development that went with it. Men are still imprisoned in the role of breadwinner, even though the economic benefits men provide for women are now resented rather than appreciated. The need to 'act like a man' is strongly imprinted – and for the most part such demeanour is expected by women also – but the pressures it produces are intense. The idea that males are privileged, Goldberg say, flies in the face of all the statistics of personal damage: in respect of longevity, proneness to disease, suicide, crime, accidents, alcoholism and drug addiction, women are on average more favoured than men.

> The man who in moments of honest reflection asks himself, 'What is in all of this for me? What am I getting, and what can I expect in the future?' may find himself at a considerable loss to answer positively or optimistically. Her changes in combination with his own rigidity have put him up against the wall. If he persists in his old ways, he stands accused of chauvinism and sexism. If he stretches himself to take on new responsibilities without making equal demands and throwing off parts of his traditional harness, he will only find himself overloaded and strained to the breaking-point. If he lets go of the traditional masculine style completely, he may find to his terror that he is becoming invisible, unsexy and unworthy in the eyes of most women and even most other men, who turn away from a man who is without a job, status and power.[10]

In contemporary relationships, according to Goldberg, men frequently find themselves in a no-win situation. Women will say 'you are afraid of closeness and emotional warmth', which is often true; but they have in fact actively sought out men they could look up to, self-contained, controlled and dedicated to the world of work. Women become angered by the very characteristics which attracted them in the first place, for they have come to devalue the forms of care which men have been most able to provide.[11]

The feminist riposte sees all this in quite a different way. According to Barbara Ehrenreich, men began a rebellion against their pre-existing gender roles some while before women.[12] Up to some thirty or forty years ago it was generally expected that a man would get married and support a wife; anyone who did not do so was regarded as in some way suspect. At a certain point, however, men became wary of being drawn into marriage and meeting its economic demands. They retained an orientation towards economic success, but no longer necessarily believed that they should work on behalf of others. To stay free, a man should stay single; he could enjoy the fruits of his work without the social requirement of a wife or established home. In Ehrenreich's view, beatniks and hippies, who appeared to place in question the life of the hard-working, conventional male, further reinforced the changes already under way, for they scorned marriage, home and domestic responsibility.

Medicine and psychology, Ehrenreich says, unwittingly contributed to the male rebellion; they showed how men were disproportionately affected by the stresses and strains of modern life. In the nineteenth century, men's life expectancy was higher than that of women; as heart disease, cancer and other illnesses replaced the previous major afflictions, like tuberculosis or pneumonia, and as death in childbirth became uncommon, women started on average to outlive men. Men have become the weaker sex and in some medical circles at least this fact was explained in terms of their need to work harder than women. Coronary heart disease, in particular, concentrated more among men than women, came to be regarded as an expression of the stresses men face. Goldberg's arguments are here turned on their head: 'the long-term effect of the coronary scare was to undermine women's claims to a share of the husband's wage and, beyond that, to indict the breadwinning role as a "lethal trap" for men.'[13]

What is the outcome? Goldberg's position, in Ehrenreich's view, allows men to try for a double gain. They can shed the breadwinner role without relinquishing their superior economic advantages as compared with women. The 'mask of masculinity' can be removed and at the same time the male can avoid any long-term domestic engagement, concentrating instead upon his own pleasures. A social climate has been created which endorses 'irresponsibility, self-indulgence and an isolationist detachment from the claims of others'.[14] Men have won their freedom while women still await theirs. The economic independence obtained by men has not become available to women, who have had to take over the responsibilities which men have shed. Women, particularly those heading single-parent families, make up a high proportion of the poor. Men have renegued on the pact that in an earlier era was the basis of the family wage.

The separation of the sexes

Given the discrepancy of their analyses, it is not surprising that the practical remedies each author offers are different. Ehrenreich's programme is primarily economic in character. Women should have a sufficient minimum income to provide for a family wage without the necessary assistance of men, which means, among other things, equality of opportunity in the labour market. Provision for child care, vocational training and government support for women without paid employment are also needed. Ehrenreich contemplates the possibility that this might mean that women tend progressively to give up on men; men will move transiently through the lives of women, who will remain the real bedrock of the family. A reconciliation between the sexes is possible, based upon 'some renewal of loyalty and trust between adult men and women', but it is far from guaranteed.[15]

Goldberg's recommendations are almost all about self-identity. Men are enjoined to redefine masculinity so as to overcome those influences that have separated them from their 'inner experience'. They must avoid the labels that have served to sustain a slavish adherence to the perform-ance principle – the worry of being thought a coward, weak, a failure, immature, impotent or a misogynist. They should cultivate close friendships with other men in order to provide the same sort of support which women are able to offer to one another. It is important for every man to break with the idea that women with whom he becomes involved should be passive and adoring; rather, he should expect to develop relationships with women who are autonomous individuals. Men need to develop their 'feminine side' and 'reclaim emotions, dependency needs, passivity, fluidity, playfulness, sensuality, vulnerability and resistance to always assuming responsibility'.[16] Do not seek so fervently to change the world, Goldberg advises men: change yourself first.

There is little doubt that new emotional antagonisms are opening up between the sexes. The sources of both male and female rage bite even more deeply than either of the foregoing accounts suggests. The phallus is only the penis: what a numbing and disconcerting discovery this is for both sexes! The claims to power of maleness depend upon a dangling piece of flesh that has now lost its distinctive connection to reproduction. This is a new castration indeed; women can now see men, at least on a cognitive level, as just as much a functionless appendage as the male sexual organ itself.

For the male, as indicated earlier, sustaining basic trust is from infancy bound up with mastery and control, including self-control, these originating in a repressed emotional dependence upon women. The need to neutralise such repressed desires, or to destroy the object of them, jostles with the requirement for love. In these circumstances, men are likely to drift away from women in large numbers and to regard commitment as equivalent to entrapment, while levels of male violence against women may very well climb beyond those currently observed.

Ambivalent dependence, however, is not confined to the male sex. Shame-fuelled rage is characteristic of female psychosexual development also. The transmuting of the phallus into the penis has troubling implications for women, because its role as a signifier of autonomy is important to their own sense of self-integrity. Female admiration of men presumes that the male is able to escape the dominance of the mother; women's complicity derives from that specific 'badness' which can be tamed by love. Many women are likely to long precisely for the kind of man who won't commit; indeed, an aversion to commitment, for reasons already explained, often maximises both his attractiveness and the challenge he offers.

All these things have a profound impact upon heterosexual ties. Heterosexual marriage superfically appears to retain its central position in the social order, making the prior discussion of lesbian relationships at best rather marginal. In reality, it has been largely undermined by the rise of the pure relationship and plastic sexuality. If orthodox marriage is not yet widely seen as just one life-style among others, as in fact it has become, this is partly the result of institutional lag and partly the result of the complicated mixture of attraction and repulsion which the psychic development of each sex creates with regard to the other. The more the pure relationship becomes the prototypical form of personal life, the more this paradoxical set of attitudes comes plainly into view. It produces various forms of dependence, and codependence, but it also has the schismatic consequences noted above.

Some marriages may still be contracted, or sustained, mainly for the sake of producing, or bringing up, children. Yet the presence of children – in 'first families' or in stepfamilies – serves as often to introduce strains in a relationship as to shore it up. Most heterosexual marriages (and many homosexual liaisons) which do not approximate to the pure relationship are likely to devolve in two directions if they do not lapse into codependence. One is a version of companionate marriage. The level of sexual involvement of the spouses with each other is low, but some degree of equality and mutual sympathy is built into the relationship. This is marriage of a late modern type, organised in terms of a model of friendship. The other form is where marriage is used as a home base by both partners, who have only a slight emotional investment in one another. This differs from the old 'standard type' of heterosexual marriage, in which the male used marriage as a place from which to operate, while the wife organised the means for his settled existence. Here both partners treat the marriage as a relatively secure environment from which they issue out to face the wider world.[17]

Yet each of these types is also likely to veer towards the pure relationship, within the life-experience of the individual and in society at large. Whether or not the sexes will grow together or apart will depend upon how far pure relationships can be contracted and carried on in a durable way. The perspectives represented by Goldberg and Ehrenreich each have their shortcomings. Ehrenreich brings together a diversity of sources in her interpretation of the increasing irresponsibility of men. The *Playboy* philosophy is discussed in the same breath as beatnik bohemia, cardiology, Maslow's psychology of human potential and attempts to found men's movements along the lines that Goldberg advocates. All move in the direction of 'mounting perfidy' as men consolidate their freedom at the expense of women. But matters are surely more complex than her account suggests. Currents of narcissism characterise some of the trends described, but so too do attempts to develop views of masculinity which run counter to male dominance. As formulated by Goldberg and others, for instance, male liberationism acknowledges the equality of women and men and argues that the ties between masculinity and economic instrumentality should be dissolved. What Ehrenreich describes as a 'flight from commitment' on the part of men actually coincides with the very beginning of 'commitment' in its current sense, a shift in sexual relations towards the emergence of the pure relationship. And this is a phenomenon with mixed consequences for men, not just for women – especially if men's covert emotional dependence upon women be recognised.

Goldberg, on the other hand, underestimates the strength of the economic and social constraints which keep women from achieving parity in the private or public domains – something connected above all with the fact that women remain the main parenting agents and domestic caretakers. Patriarchy remains entrenched throughout the social and economic order. He also underplays the force of the psychic resistances which affect the behaviour of men and women, as well as the contradictory character of psychosexual formations. 'Why can't a good man be sexy; why can't a sexy man be good?' – this is a plea from the heart, not just a quixotic feminine refusal to accept the full implications of gender equality. It has a very real counterpart in men's proclivity for episodic sexuality, for reasons discussed earlier.

No one knows how far the advent of the pure relationship will prove more explosive than integrating in its consequences. The transformation of intimacy, together with plastic sexuality, provides for conditions which could bring about a reconciliation of the sexes. More is involved, however, than greater economic equality and psychic restructuring, extremely difficult to achieve though these may be. I shall try to show why in the concluding chapters.

NOTES

1 All quotations in the preceding paragraphs are from Shere Hite: *Women and Love*, London: Viking, 1988.
2 Charlotte Wolff: *Bisexuality*, London: Quartet, 1979.
3 Hite in *Women and Love* actually discusses this phenomenon twice in her book, on p. 610 and p. 641, apparently without noticing the repetition. The figures given for women who remain close friends with their ex-lovers are slightly different in the two places, 64 per cent on one page and 62 per cent on the other.
4 Hite: *Women and Love*.
5 Sydney Abbott and Barbara Love: *Sappho Was a Right-On Woman*, New York: Stein, 1977, p. 74.
6 Martin Hoffman: *The Gay World*, New York: Basic, 1968, pp. 49–50.
7 Heather Formani: *Men. The Darker Continent*, London: Mandarin, 1991, pp. 23–30.
8 Hite: *Women and Love*, p. 73.
9 Herb Goldberg: *The Hazards of Being Male*, New York: Signet, 1976; *The New Male*, New York: Signet, 1979; and other works by the same author.
10 Goldberg: *The Hazards of Being Male*, p. 3.
11 Goldberg: *The New Male*, p. 163.
12 Barbara Ehrenreich: *The Hearts of Men*, London: Pluto, 1983.
13 Ibid., p. 86.
14 Ibid., p. 169.
15 Ibid., p. 182.
16 Goldberg: *The New Male*, p. 254.
17 For a somewhat different typology, see Hite: *Women and Love*, pp. 521–3.

9

SEXUALITY, REPRESSION, CIVILISATION

Is sexuality, in some sense or another, the key to modern civilisation? Many, mostly from the progressive side of the political spectrum, have answered in the affirmative. According to the usual interpretations at least – although these are surely inadequate – Freud would be something of an exception, since he connected his view of sexuality to a conservative view of modern civilisation. Followers of Freud, however, have often adapted his ideas, or certain of them, to radical ends. Modern civilisation is repressive, yes, but the release of sexual expression from its constraints could produce emancipation of a far-reaching sort. Sex, as Edward Carpenter said, 'goes first, and hands eyes mouth brain follow; from the midst of belly and thighs radiates the knowledge of self, religion and immortality'.[1]

Sex and repression: Reich

> Ye specious worthies who scoff at me
> Whence thrives your politics
> As long as ye have ruled the world?
> From dagger thrusts and murder!

Thus begins Wilhelm Reich's *Listen, Little Man!*, a book whose very title echoes a paranoiac aggressiveness which runs through the text, but which also defends a vision of radical social reform that Reich pursued for the whole of his life.[2] For the bold way in which he challenged authority, Reich was persecuted by a variety of groups, ranging from psychoanalytic orthodoxy, religious organisations and the US government through to those he decried as 'red fascists'. The first, and most famous, of the psychoanalytic sexual radicals, Reich saw his ideas traduced by all of these groups and more besides.

Reich was the scourge of bourgeois marriage and saw in genital sexuality – its frustration or cultivation – the clue to the ailments of modernity. The 'little man' to whom Reich addresses himself is indeed a member of the male sex, but not just the average man in the street; he is all those, including people in positions of power, who are slaves to convention, neurotics believing themselves to be healthy. The little man, Reich says, not mincing his words, is 'miserable and small, stinking, impotent, rigid, lifeless and empty'. He is his own slave-driver, compelled by his own anxieties to seek to prevent others from claiming their freedom.

The neurosis of the little man Reich traced to the damming up of sexual energy; but he was far from propagating the uncontrolled sexual licence of which his enemies accused him:

'You are a Miserable Little Man!' he proclaimed.

You run your automobiles and trains over the bridges which the great Galileo invented. Do you know, Little Man, that the great Galileo had three children, without a marriage licence? That you don't tell your school children. And, did you not torture Galileo for this reason also? . . .

You have no inkling of the fact that it is your pornographic

mind and your sexual irresponsibility which put you in the
shackles of your marriage laws . . .

You have no woman, or if you have one, you only want to
'lay' her in order to prove the 'man' in you. You don't know
what love is . . .

You know, and I know, and everybody knows, that you
go around in a perpetual state of sexual starvation; that you
look greedily at every member of the other sex; that you talk
with your friends about love in terms of dirty jokes . . . One
night, I heard you and your friends walk along the street,
yelling in unison: 'We want women! We want women!'[3]

Reich opposed sexuality to power, and saw in the reign
of the 'little man' the origins of that authoritarianism he so
vehemently resisted. Sexuality, appropriately expressed, is
our main source of happiness and whoever is happy is free
from the thirst for power. Someone who has a 'feeling of
living life' has an autonomy which comes from nurturing
the potentialities of the self. Sexuality oriented to the 'loving
embrace' provides a way beyond domination – a route, as
Reich puts it, to freedom from the constraints of unmastered
sexual desire. In the place of 'driven sexuality', the sexuality
which seeks 'to pinch every waitress in the behind', people
should become 'openly happy in their love'.[4]

How can such a situation be brought about? Not just by
political reform, Reich says, but by the reform of mass
character. For Reich, character is a defensive formation, a
protective 'armour' developed to withstand the vicissitudes
of life. Character he describes as a chronic deformation of
the ego, which takes the form of a rigidity. The armour a
person develops protects against external and internal dan-
gers, although at great psychic cost; it develops as a result
of the blocking of libido. The 'hardening of the ego' results
from various sets of processes. The identification with a
frustrating reality or, more specifically, individuals who
represent this reality gives the armouring its meaningful

content. Aggression, generated by the frustrating other, produces anxiety which is turned against the self; an individual's energies are thus blocked from motor expression and become inhibitions. Such energies become drawn in to the warding off of sexual impulses, which surface only in a compulsive way.

Reich's therapeutic method involves piercing the character armour by undermining the 'neurotic equilibrium' of the individual. For many people, the capacity for spontaneous enjoyment, which has its origins in sexual pleasure, has become distorted by sadism, greed and selfishness. Character is a mark of insincerity which, however, can become changed in such a way as to produce happiness. The neurotic equilibrium can be broken through by freeing libido from pregenital fixations. During the course of therapy, infant genital anxiety is reactivated, but as a means of re-establishing 'orgastic potency' lost as a result of distorted psychosexual development.[5]

According to Reich, Freud wrote *Civilisation and Its Discontents* in some part as a refutation of the 'danger' presented by Reich's interpretation of modernity.[6] In Reich's view, Freud mistakenly equated modern institutions with civilisation in general. Anticipating the path later charted by Marcuse, Reich argues that modern culture is specifically repressive; but he rejects the idea of the death instinct, arguing that destructiveness results from frustrated libido. Freud had deliberately sought to undermine the possibilities of sexual liberation by blocking off the radical implications of his own ideas.[7]

There is some truth in the assertion. As against Foucault's thesis that Freud epitomises the modern preoccupation with sexuality, in his later writings Freud deliberately set out to modify his earlier, 'exaggerated' emphasis upon libido. His lead was followed by the majority of the members of the psychoanalytic profession, even where they rejected the conception of the death instinct. Reich saw himself as a

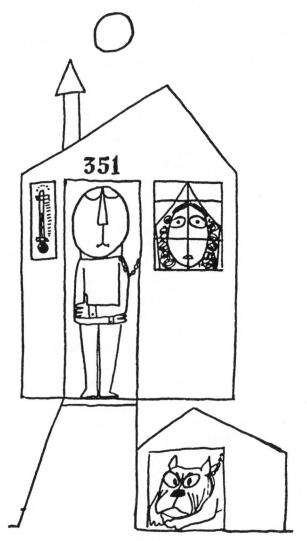

You beg for happiness, but security is more important to you
from Wilhelm Reich *Listen, Little Man*, London, Souvenir Press, 1972.

defender of a true faith. Modern society is patriarchal and its emphasis upon monogamous marriage serves to develop authoritarian traits of character, thereby supporting an exploitative social system. Behind this phenomenon stands a crucial transition in early history, from a matriarchal society in which the repression of infantile and adolescent sexuality was unknown.

Reich believed that sociopolitical reform without sexual liberation is impossible: freedom and sexual health are the same thing. While he advocated equality of sexual expression for women, he gave particular attention to the sexual rights of children and adolescents. Children are to be given the right to engage in sexual play with others and to masturbate; they are also to be protected from the domination of their parents. Adolescents are to have the opportunity to fulfil their sexual needs in an unbridled way, in order that they might be the agents of future social change. Homosexuality Reich regarded as the product of thwarted libido; he considered that it will disappear with the progressive liberation of sexuality – as will pornography.

The later work of Reich has been seen by many as bizarre, the ideas of a person who towards the end of his life himself became deranged. Yet its direction of development is important, and there are in fact strong continuities between his earlier and later writings. Reich was long suspicious of Freud's talking cure. Free association, according to Reich, often leads away from a person's problems rather than helping to disclose them. The body and its dispositions, he came to see, have their own expressive language; in order to get a true evaluation of an individual, the therapist should ask him or her *not* to speak for a while. 'For as soon as the patient ceases to talk, the bodily expression of emotion becomes clearly manifest.' 'Orgone therapy' is based on promoting sexual expressiveness through the genital orgasm. The underlying aim, however, is to allow the individual to express her- or himself somatically, in such a way that 'language is eliminated to a far-reaching degree'.[8] Reich's idea that sexual energy becomes imprisoned in the individual's musculature carries residues of nineteenth-century views of hysteria, but also anticipates the arrival of 'stress' as a physical pathology later in the present century. More significantly, reflexive control of the body is recognised as being at the centre of psychological difficulties. There is no confessional here: Reich abandoned the talking cure in favour of programmes of relaxation, massage and the dissipation of bodily tension.

Herbert Marcuse

Marcuse also sought to discern 'the hidden trend in psychoanalysis' towards radicalism.[9] Critical of Erich Fromm and other 'revisionists', Marcuse tried like Reich to lay bare the liberative potential in Freud's work. Libido is rescued, but the death instinct is sustained as a sobering reminder of the limits to pure pleasure. All civilisation presumes 'basic repression' of the life and death drives, but in modern society the demands of economic discipline introduce an historical, and dispensable, burden of repression. In adjusting to Freud's 'reality principle', the individual is in fact responding to the exigencies of a form of exploitative domination.

Marcuse's interpretation of Freud has something in common with the Lacanian version, although the end-result is very different. Like Lacan, Marcuse criticises ego psychology, and places a strong emphasis upon the unconscious. In contrast to Lacan, however, Marcuse believes that a recovery of the unconscious offers a powerful medium for radical social criticism; for Marcuse, this is because ego psychology accepts the world as it is. By turning to the instincts, in Freud's sense of that term, we can lay bare mechanisms of social repression and we can also give a content to the emancipatory promise of modernity.

The key conceptual moves in Marcuse's diagnosis of the possibility of emancipation are the division of repression into basic and surplus repression and the adding of the performance principle to the reality principle. Some forms of repression, in other words, result from the 'innerwordly asceticism' of modern institutions, and can be dispelled when those institutions are transcended. They are 'surplus to requirements' in a psychological sense. The performance principle is the principle implied in facing, not 'reality' as such, but the (impermanent) historical reality of a particular social order. What Marcuse describes as the 'monogamic-patriarchal' family, for example, is one social form where there is a surplus of repression. However, he concentrates by far the bulk of his attention upon surplus repression in the context of the workplace.

Emancipation for Marcuse is linked to the primacy of pleasure, which he sharply differentiates from hedonism. Modern work discipline is only possible to the degree that the body is de-eroticised; if libido were allowed to escape surplus repression, it would threaten or destroy that discipline completely. Hedonism, Marcuse affirms in one of his early writings, 'embodies a correct judgement about society'. The pursuit of the sensuous strikes at the heart of surplus repression and thus has an inherently critical edge. Hedonism, nevertheless, is anarchic and is only emancipatory if linked to truth. Truth in this sense appears quite distinct from Foucault's conception of the 'truth' of sexuality: it is pleasure realigned with norms of happiness and aesthetic appreciation. For happiness, Marcuse agrees with Plato, is pleasure 'subjected to the criterion of truth'.[10]

In an interesting passage of *Civilisation and Its Discontents*, Marcuse points out, Freud connects the repressive character of civilisation, not to the sublimation of the instincts as such, but to the exclusiveness of sexual relationships. 'Sexual love', Freud says, 'is a relationship between two people in which a third can only be superfluous or disturbing.'[11] A pair of lovers has no interest in anyone else; civilisation cannot tolerate this, because it depends upon relations between larger groups of persons. Freud here reproduces, as it were, the traditional objection to *amour passion*. Yet, as Marcuse quite properly observes, sexual love can be liberating in a double sense: when harnessed to respect for the other as an equal, love shatters the framework of the monogamic-patriarchal family, but also is positively compatible with wider social citizenship. 'Free Eros' is not only consistent with, but the very condition of, 'lasting civilised societal relationships'.[12]

Marcuse constantly uses Freud against himself to demonstrate that Freud's interpretation of the psychic demands of modernity is as revolutionary as it is conservative. Thus Freud says that primary narcissism survives in modern civilisation, not only as neurosis, but as something of an 'alternative reality'. Especially, although not exclusively, in relation to sexuality, narcissism can generate an oceanic feeling of 'oneness with the universe'. Narcissism, usually understood (and one could add here, not only by Freud, but by current cultural critics like Christopher Lash, as well as by Foucault in his picture of the 'Californian cult of the self') as a defensive adaptation to the wider world through withdrawal from it, reveals a potential for transcendence. Narcissism 'may become the source and reservoir for a new libidinal cathexis of the objective world – transforming this world into a new mode of being'.[13]

Marcuse differs sharply from Reich in his evaluation of the nature of genital sexuality. Freud proposed, Marcuse says, that the sexual excitation of the child takes the form of a generalised bodily eroticism, which later becomes focused upon the genitals as a normal process of psychosexual development. (Actually, as noted in Chapter 7, Freud stated that a focusing upon genital sexuality is characteristic of boys; girls are forced to 'make do' with a more diffuse eroticism.) In Marcuse's view, Freud failed to see that the progression towards genital sexuality is a restriction upon the possibilities of pleasure imposed by the modern social order. 'Genital tyranny' results from the fact that libido has been stripped away from the parts of the body needed to participate in industrial labour. A resexualising of the body, together with a renewal of the original meaning of eroticism, which is linked to aesthetic appreciation, is called for as part of future revolutionary change. Marcuse does not fully endorse plastic sexuality, but instead regards 'perversions', including homosexuality, as behavioural critiques of the regime of genital sexuality. They mark sites of resistance to the subjugation of sexual activity to procreation.[14]

For Marcuse, as for Freud, the death instinct is not a wholly destructive force. Human creativity is a consequence of a fusion of life and death instincts, and the problem with modern civilisation is that the death instinct has become detached from its necessary interaction with libidinal energy. Thanatos has become incorporated into the rigid, mechanical character of modern discipline, which permeates more than only the workplace. The overcoming of alienated labour will release surplus repression and also reconnect the death instinct with the sources of sexual pleasure. Release from toil allows for the re-eroticising, not only of the body, but of nature. For the pre-eminence of genital sexuality is associated with an instrumental outlook towards the natural environment. 'Non-repressive sublimation' would be a basis for a renewed harmony with nature.[15]

A non-repressive culture – one sustaining only basic repression – Marcuse argues, would be in some part regressive, in a psychic sense. It would be a reversal of civilisation which is at the same time an overcoming, a going back in order to progress forward. Liberated from 'sex', Eros has culture-building capacities well beyond those available in present-day society. So far as political theory goes, Charles Fourrier has more to teach us than Marx. Pleasurable co-operation based upon *attraction passionée*, not passionate love but the flowering of Eros in communicative love and friendship, would become the dominant medium of sociability. In Marcuse's words, 'With the transformation from sexuality into Eros, the life instincts evolve their sensuous order, while reason becomes sensuous to the degree to which it comprehends and organises necessity in terms of protecting and enriching the life instincts . . . repressive reason gives way to a new *rationality of gratification* in which reason and happiness converge.'[16]

The possibilities of sexual radicalism

A major source of difficulty for anyone who, like Reich and Marcuse, says that modern civilisation is inherently repressive is that very public fascination with sex which Foucault notes. The maturation of modern institutions is not associated with the increasing constraint, but with its growing prominence almost everywhere. Marcuse was aware of the issue and had an answer. Sexual permissiveness is not at all the same as liberation. The commodifying of sexuality is pervasive, but eroticism is more or less thoroughly expunged from view. The antagonism with which sexuality was regarded in earlier phases of the development of the West is actively preferable, Marcuse argues, to 'sexual freedom' which conceals its oppressiveness beneath a gloss of enjoyment. Previously an awareness of what was disbarred was preserved; we may seem freer, but are in fact living in subjection.

Who defends the ideas of Reich and Marcuse today? Very few and it is instructive to ask why. Foucault might claim that, like their mentor, Freud, they were taken in by the repressive hypothesis. Each believed that modern societies depend upon a high level of sexual repression, signalled first of all in Victorianism. They were wrong in this supposition and therefore the rest of their ideas are suspect. Yet the repressive hypothesis aside, the gap between the views of Reich and Marcuse, and Foucault, is not as wide as might be thought. Repressive desublimation is not a term Foucault would use and is alien to his thought; but for him as for the others the permissiveness of the present era is a phenomenon of power and is not a pathway to emancipation. 'Perhaps one day', Foucault muses, 'there will be a different economy of bodies and pleasures.'[17] Marcuse and Reich would agree, although both had a rather fuller view of how this might come about than Foucault chose to elaborate.

To grasp the limitations (and also what seems to me the persistent importance) of the views of the 'sexual radicals' we have to look elsewhere than to Foucault. In the writings of Reich and Marcuse, little is said about gender, or about changes influencing the development of love relations in the modern social order. Reich wrote a good deal about love, as well as about the patriarchal family. Following Freud in this respect, at least, he argued that the good life would be built around the 'three pillars' of love, work and knowledge. Yet neither in his work nor in that of Marcuse do we find any systematic theory of gender and love as themselves revolutionary influences. Sexuality is usually described as though it were androgynous, a direct result of following a conception of libido that is anonymous in respect of gender. Marcuse simply seemed to ignore Freud's analysis of the different paths of psychosexual development. While both Reich and Marcuse were enthusiastic supporters of the women's movement, neither built into their writings an interpretation of the impact of the struggles of women in the domestic environment or elsewhere. The omission of a concern with love is a puzzling feature of Marcuse's work – although a moment's reflection will remind the reader that such an absence is characteristic of most versions of social theory. The troubles of modernity which Marcuse stresses for the most part are very much those of a male-dominated domain. Love, one has to presume, is once more somewhere behind the scenes as that specialisation of women which in fact it became. In the foreground there is only the world of paid labour, taken for granted as a male enterprise. Is it surprising that the burdens of modernity, as depicted by Marcuse, resonate strongly with 'damaged masculinity' as interpreted by Goldberg and others?

Marcuse has no explanation of the origins of the sexual permissiveness that he excoriates. Nor, it seems to me, has Reich, or indeed anyone who begins from Freud's theory of civilisation and repression, however much it is radicalised. For radicalising Freud means showing that what he took to be characteristics of civilisation in general are really specific to the modern order. That order is presented as much more monolithic, and resistant to change, than it really is. If modern institutions in fact depended upon sexual repression, this should increase, not decline, with their further development. To say that 'permissiveness' is a distorted form of sexuality provides a label for a process of increased liberalisation, but does not explain how it could have occurred. Moreover, these thinkers do not see in such liberalisation a sign of progress; an increase in sexual licence does not threaten the edifice which entombs us in the all-enveloping disciplinary system.

Foucault has as his very starting-point the Western pre-occupation with sex, and in addition casts doubt on the idea of repression. Concern with sexuality, including the invention of 'sexuality' itself, is an outcome of the spread of surveillance as a means of generating power. Such power was early on concentrated upon the body as a machine – shades of Max Weber and even Marcuse here – and later upon biological processes affecting reproduction, health and longevity. Modern societies are not based, as were pre-modern systems, on the power to take life, but upon the power to develop it, 'to invest life through and through'.[18] The former influence, one could say, marks Foucault's acceptance of the asceticism in which modern social life is supposedly steeped. The 'contact between life and history', as Foucault puts it, which represents the second element, is something else again. For millennia human beings lived under the imprint of nature. The natural environment held sway over human activity; demographic growth was largely governed by the vagaries of nature. From about the eighteenth century onwards, however, these processes were increasingly subjected to human control.

Sex became such a pre-eminent concern, according to Foucault, because it formed the main connecting point between these two influences over bodily development. It 'was a means of access both to the life of the body and the life of the species'. This is why 'sexuality was sought out in the smallest details of individual existences; it was tracked down in behaviour, pursued in dreams; it was suspected of underlying the least follies, it was traced back into the earliest years of childhood'.[19] The deployment of sexuality as power made sex a mystery but also, in Foucault's view, constituted 'sex' as something desirable, in which we must engage to establish our individuality. Reich's critique of sexual repression, for Foucault, was the prisoner of that which it sought to liberate. The very fact that so many shifts in sexual behaviour have occurred since the nineteenth century, without being accompanied by the other changes Reich anticipated, indicates that this 'antirepressive' struggle is part of the field of sexuality, not a subversion of it.[20]

Yet Foucault's own view, already criticised in Chapter 2, is wanting. What Foucault terms power – that 'power' which mysteriously does things of its own volition – was in some fundamental respects gender power. It was women who were de-energised, taken out of modernity's core arenas, their capability for sexual enjoyment denied – at the very same time at which they were beginning to construct an infrastructural revolution. Love, together with that affective individualism of which Lawrence Stone speaks, was at the centre of the changes in family organisation, and was also important in other transformations affecting intimate life. These changes did not originate with the state, or from administrative power in a more general sense. If it be accepted, as it must be, that power is distributive as well as generative, we can say that they derived not from power but from lack of it.

Foucault offers a specific interpretation of why the constraining form of biopower was succeeded by the more dynamic one. The first was dominated by the requirement to create a compliant labour force; the second corresponded to a later phase of development in the twentieth century in which labour power no longer had to be subjected to the same degree of direct control. Once such a transition had been effected, sexuality became channelled into a diversity of social circuits and thereby more or less all-pervasive.

This idea is surely not convincing, even if it relates only to sexual behaviour as narrowly understood, let alone to changes affecting personal relationships more generally. It suggests that our fascination with sex derives from the sheer expansion of sexuality as a discursive phenomenon, which enters areas where previously it was absent. I don't believe that biopower, such as Foucault describes it, explains changes in sexual attitudes and outlooks described in earlier chapters. Such changes are at least in some part a result of struggle and it is impossible to deny that there are emancipatory elements involved. Not emancipation, perhaps, exactly in the manner envisaged by Reich or Marcuse, but not merely a grapple with an entangling spider's web such as Foucault proposes. Women in particular have achieved sexual freedoms which, however partial they may still be, are remarkable compared with even a few short decades ago. Whatever the limitations and distortions to which it is subject, there is far more open dialogue about sexuality, in which virtually the whole population is involved, than would have seemed conceivable to earlier generations.

Institutional repression and the question of sexuality

Let us therefore rethink the relation between sexuality and power, beginning from the assertion that power, as such, does nothing. The generative aspects of power, like its distributive characteristics, are bound up with specific properties of social organisation, with the activities of situated groups and individuals, as well as with varying contexts and modes of institutional reflexivity. Sexuality was not created by 'power', nor is the pervasiveness of sexuality, in any direct way at least, the result of its focal importance for such 'power'.

In my view, there is no such thing as biopower, at least in the generic sense in which Foucault conceives of it. Instead, we can distinguish several threads of organisational and personal transformation in the development of modern societies. The administrative development of modern institutions should be separated from the socialisation of nature and reproduction – fundamental processes, and directly related to sexuality, but not to be analysed in the manner suggested by Foucault. These in turn should be distinguished from the reflexive project of the self and the innovations in personal life linked to it.

As regards the impact of surveillance, one can agree with Foucault that sexuality, like most other aspects of personal life, has become thoroughly caught up in, and restructured by, the expansion of power systems. Modern organisations, including the state, penetrate local activities in ways that were unknown in pre-modern cultures. Discourses of science – including social science – have been directly embroiled in these processes. Yet as stated earlier, the creation of administrative power is much more of a dialectical phenomenon than Foucault admits. Spaces for mobilisation and countervailing power are produced by the very expansion of surveillance. A society of developed institutional reflexivity is a highly charged one, making possible forms of personal and collective engagement which very substantially alter the sexual domain.

The characteristic movement of modernity, it can be argued, is towards the creation of internally referential systems – orders of activity determined by principles internal to themselves.[21] Certain distinctive areas of social life in pre-modern cultures tended to be governed by 'external' influences (sometimes stabilised as taken for granted phenomena by tradition, but including also biological and physical factors). With the advent of modern institutions, however, these became more and more subject to social intervention. Thus the invention of 'deviance' socialised a miscellaneous set of external characteristics, among them poverty, vagabondage and madness, all of which once upon a time were taken as natural parameters of existence, as 'given by the will of God'. Deviance was socially constituted and at the same time separated from the main arenas of social activity, through a process of sequestration. Similarly, sickness and death, once 'limiting points' of the influence of the biological upon the social, became increasingly socialised and concealed from view.

Sequestered nature and sexuality are connected in a crucial way through the socialisation of reproduction. While modern contraception is the most obvious technological expression of reproduction as an internally referential system, it is not its original impetus. This has its main source in the very separation of reproduction from Malthusian conditions which Foucault mentions.[22] Once family size starts to be carefully limited – something which develops mainly from within the family itself – reproduction comes to be governed primarily by the desire to rear children as an autonomous concern. The inventioon of childhood and of motherhood have their origins here. 'Sexuality' had no distinct existence so long as sexual behaviour was bound up with reproduction and with the generations. Sexual activity was divided up between an orientation to reproduction and the *ars erotica* – that split which also classified women into the pure and the impure.

Sexuality becomes a property of the individual the more the life-span becomes internally referential and the more self-identity is grasped as a reflexively organised endeavour. As it is constituted as such a domain, sexuality also retreats behind the scenes, sequestered from view in a physical as well as in a social sense. It is now a means of forging connections with others on the basis of intimacy, no longer grounded in an immutable kinship order sustained across the generations. Passion is secularised, taken out of *amour passion*, and reorganised as the romantic love complex; it is privatised and redefined.

What can be termed 'the sequestration of experience'[23] is a consequence of the ever-more radical break of the institutions of modernity with tradition, and the growing intrusion of its systems of control across pre-existing 'external boundaries' of social action. It has as its consequence the dissolution of the moral and ethical lineaments which related social activity to the transcendental, to nature and to reproduction. These are exchanged, in effect, for the security in routine which modern social life offers. A sense of ontological security comes primarily from routine itself; the individual is morally and psychologically vulnerable whenever established routines are broken through. Given what has been said so far, it is clear that such vulnerability is not neutral in respect of gender.

Sequestration is a form of repression, a 'forgetting', but it does not presume an ever-increasing burden of guilt. Instead, mechanisms of shame, linked to the reflexive project of self, interlace with, although they do not wholly replace, those involving guilt anxiety. A rising propensity to the experience of shame – the feeling that one is worthless, one's life empty and one's body an inadequate device – follows upon the spread of modernity's internally referential systems. The reflexive project of self, which carries so many possibilities for autonomy and happiness, has to be undertaken in the context of routines largely devoid of ethical content. Sexual activity is liable to be dogged by that 'emptiness', that search for an ever-elusive sense of completion, which affects both sexes, although in different ways. For many men, this is a restless search to overcome the sentiments of inadequacy which so deeply wound the little boy who must forsake his mother. For women much more prominent is that 'quest romance' for the desired but unavailable father. In both cases, however, there is a longing for love.

Modernity as obsessional

We should pause at this point to consider what it might actually mean to say that there is a general preoccupation with sexuality in modern culture. One interpretation, somewhat in the manner of Marcuse, might look to commodification as the prime domain in which such a preoccupation is evident. Sexuality generates pleasure; and pleasure, or at least the promise of it, provides a leverage for marketing goods in a capitalistic society. Sexual imagery appears almost everywhere in the marketplace as a sort of gigantic selling ploy; the commodifying of sex, it might be argued, is a means of diverting the mass of the population from their true needs, whatever these are thought to be. The prominence of sexuality might then be interpreted in terms of a movement from a capitalistic order, dependent upon labour, discipline and self-denial, to one concerned to foster consumerism and therefore hedonism.

The limitations of such an idea, however, are obvious enough. It does not explain why sexuality should have the prominence it does; if sex is a powerful adjunct to consumerism, it must be because a driving concern with it already exists. Moreover, there is plenty of evidence to the effect that sexuality is worrying, disturbing, fraught with tensions. Pleasure is hedged about with too many countervailing tendencies to make plausible the idea that sexuality forms the centrepoint of a hedonistic consumer society.

Another view might draw once more on Foucault. Sex would be our 'truth', the core of a generalised confessional principle of modern civilisation. I have already suggested reasons why this view will not do on the level of analysis; taken as a descriptive characteristic of modern culture it is also quite unconvincing. Freud's thought was immediately challenged by other therapies which questioned the decisive importance he attributed to sex. The idea of 'sex as truth' has made some headway, but one could hardly claim that it has become the energising principle of modern thought as a whole.

A third interpretation might point to the phenomenon of sex addiction. The centrality of sexuality in modern societies is indicated by the compulsive qualities of sexual behaviour today. Such compulsiveness is evident, it might be said, in widespread addiction to pornography, salacious magazines, films and other media, and in the dedicated pursuit of sexual experience to which many devote themselves. Descriptively this is more adequate, but we still have to ask what the origins of this situation are, as well as considering how such a state of affairs could come about in a society supposedly based upon sexual repression.

I think these conundrums can be solved in the following way. Sexuality became sequestered or privatised as part of the processes whereby motherhood was invented and became a basic component of the female domain. The sequestering of sexuality occurred largely as a result of social rather than psychological repression, and concerned two things above all: the confinement or denial of female sexual responsiveness and the generalised acceptance of male sexuality as unproblematic. These developments were reworkings of age-old divisions between the sexes, particularly the schism between pure and impure women, but they were recast in a new institutional format. The more sexuality became detached from reproduction, and integrated within an emerging reflexive project of self, the more this institutional system of repression came under tension.

Women became charged, *de facto*, with managing the transformation of intimacy which modernity set in train. The system of institutional repression was from the beginning subject to strain because of the exclusion of women from the public sphere. The enquiries which men carried on into the nature of women were not just an expression of traditional sexual otherness; they were investigations into unacknowledged arenas of self-identity and intimacy, as reordered areas of social life to which men had little entry. Sexuality thus did indeed become a matter of prime concern to both sexes, although in divergent ways. For women, the problem was to constitute love as a medium of communication and self-development – in relation to children as well as to men. The claiming of female sexual pleasure came to form a basic part of the reconstitution of intimacy, an emancipation as important as any sought after in the public domain. For men, sexual activity became compulsive to the degree to which it remained isolated from these more subterranean changes.

Sexual emancipation

In the wake of Foucault's work, versions of sexual emancipation have been suggested which differ markedly from those of Reich or Marcuse. For the most part these are variations on the theme of plastic sexuality. The 'biological justification' for heterosexuality as 'normal', it might be proposed, has fallen apart. What used to be called perversions are merely ways in which sexuality can legitimately be expressed and self-identity defined. Recognition of diverse sexual proclivities corresponds to acceptance of a plurality of possible life-styles, which is a political gesture:

> The speaking perverts, first given a carefully shaded public platform in the volumes of early sexologists, have become highly vocal on their own behalf. They no longer need to ventriloquise through the Latinate and literary prose of a Krafft-Ebing or Havelock Ellis, or engage in the intricate transference and counter-transference of analyst and analysed. They speak for themselves in street politics and lobbying, through pamphlets, journals and books, via the semiotics of highly sexualised settings, with their elaborate codes of keys, colours and clothes, in the popular media, and in the more mundane details of domestic life.[24]

The approach of 'radical pluralism' is an emancipatory endeavour which seeks to develop guidelines for sexual choice, but makes no claim that these represent coherent moral principles. The radical value of pluralism derives, not from its shock effects – little shocks us any more – but from the effect of recognising that 'normal sexuality' is simply one type of life-style choice among others. 'Subjective feelings, intentions and meanings are vital elements in deciding on the merits of an activity. The decisive factor is an awareness of context, of the situation in which choices are made.'[25] Sexual pluralism, its advocates argue, would not be a succumbing to sexuality, but could offer just what Foucault seems to hold out as a possibility, an overcoming of the dominance that sexuality exerts over our lives.

As it stands, however, such a programme is vague and any version of sexual liberation which emphasises only the factor of choice faces a whole battery of objections. The meaning and potentialities of sexual emancipation need to be understood in a different fashion, although acceptance of the legitimacy of plastic sexuality is certainly part of the matter. A few provisional observations might help at this point. No viewpoint which pits the energy of sexuality against the disciplinary characteristics of the modern social order is likely to be of much value. Nor is one that looks to the more eccentric or non-conventional forms of sexuality as an avant-garde, which will batter the citadels of orthodoxy until they yield. Finally, if sexual pluralism is to be embraced, it has to offer more than just a sort of casual cosmopolitanism, particularly if other issues intrinsic to sexuality, including gender difference and the ethics of the pure relationship, are not addressed.

I have argued that sexuality has the importance for us today that it does, not because of its significance for the control systems of modernity, but because it is a point of connection between two other processes: the sequestration of experience and the transformation of intimacy. The separation of sexuality from reproduction and the socialisation of reproduction develop as traditional modes of conduct, with all their moral richness – and their imbalances of gender power – become replaced by modernity's internally referential orders. At the same time as what used to be 'natural' becomes increasingly socialised, and partly as a direct result, the domains of personal activity and interaction start to become fundamentally altered. Sexuality serves as a metaphor for these changes and is the focus for their expression, particularly in respect of the reflexive project of self.

The sequestration of experience separates individuals from some of the major moral reference-points by means of which social life was ordered in pre-modern cultures. In these cultures, relations to nature and to the succession of the generations were coordinated by traditional forms of practice, and by religiously inspired ethical codes. The extension of internally referential systems shields the individual from disturbing questions raised by the existential parameters of human life, but it leaves those questions unanswered. Sexuality, it could be suggested, gains its compelling quality, together with its aura of excitement and danger, from the fact that it puts us in contact with these lost fields of experience. Its ecstasy, or the promise of it, has echoes of the 'ethical passion' which transcendental symbolism used to inspire – and of course cultivated eroticism, as distinct from sexuality in the service of reproduction, has long been associated with religiosity.

Conclusion

Few, as I have said, now read either Reich or Marcuse. Yet their respective visions of a non-repressive order retain a certain beauty and it is not at all clear that those visions should simply be consigned to oblivion. Sexuality is a terrain of fundamental political struggle and also a medium of emancipation, just as the sexual radicals claimed. A non-repressive society, as Reich and Marcuse both stress, would be one in which sexuality is increasingly freed from compulsiveness. Emancipation thus presumes autonomy of action in the context of the generalisation of plastic sexuality. It is separate from permissiveness in so far as it creates an ethics of personal life which makes possible a conjunction of happiness, love and respect for others.

The sexual radicals presumed that a double order of revolution would be necessary before we could even begin to contemplate such a state of affairs. Society would have to undergo a thorough-going upheaval, and a great deal of psychic change would also be necessary. Yet if, as I have suggested, sexual repression has above all been a matter of social sequestration coupled to gender power, something of a different slant can be put on things. We have no need to

wait around for a sociopolitical revolution to further programmes of emancipation, nor would such a revolution help
very much. Revolutionary processes are already well under
way in the infrastructure of personal life. The transformation
of intimacy presses for psychic as well as social change and
such change, going 'from the bottom up', could potentially
ramify through other, more public, institutions.

Sexual emancipation, I think, can be the medium of a
wide-ranging emotional reorganisation of social life. The
concrete meaning of emancipation in this context is not,
however, as the sexual radicals proposed, a substantive set
of psychic qualities or forms of behaviour. It is more effectively understood in a procedural way, as the possibility of
the *radical democratisation* of the personal. Who says sexual
emancipation, in my view, says sexual democracy. It is not
only sexuality at stake here. The democratisation of personal
life, as a potential, extends in a fundamental way to friendship relations and, crucially, to the relations of parents,
children and other kin.

NOTES

1 Edward Carpenter: *Selected Writings*, vol. 1: *Sex*, London: GMP,
  1984, frontispiece.
2 Wilhelm Reich: *Listen, Little Man!*, London: Souvenir, 1972.
3 Ibid., pp. 43, 61.
4 Ibid., pp. 111–12.
5 Wilhelm Reich: *Character Analysis*, London: Vision, 1950.
6 Wilhelm Reich: *The Function of the Orgasm*, New York: Farrar,
  Straus and Giroux, 1961, pp. 165–8.
7 Wilhelm Reich: *The Sexual Revolution*, New York: Farrar, Straus
  and Giroux, 1962, pp. 247ff.
8 Reich: *Character Analysis*, p. 362.
9 Herbert Marcuse: *Eros and Civilisation*, London: Allen Lane, 1970,
  p. 11.

10 Herbert Marcuse: 'On hedonism', in *Negations*, London: Allen Lane, 1968.
11 Quoted in Marcuse: *Eros and Civilisation*, p. 48.
12 Ibid., p. 49.
13 Ibid., p. 138.
14 Ibid., pp. 164–6.
15 Herbert Marcuse: *One-Dimensional Man*, London: Allen Lane, 1972.
16 Marcuse: *Eros and Civilisation*, pp. 179–80.
17 Michel Foucault: *The History of Sexuality*, vol. 1: *An Introduction*, Harmondsworth: Pelican, 1981, p. 159.
18 Ibid., pp. 139–42.
19 Ibid., p. 146.
20 Ibid., pp. 130–31.
21 Anthony Giddens: *Modernity and Self-Identity*, Cambridge: Polity, 1991, ch. 5 and *passim*.
22 Cf. Mitchell Dean: *The Constitution of Poverty*, London: Routledge, 1991.
23 Ibid.
24 Jeffrey Weeks: *Sexuality and Its Discontents*, London: Routledge, 1985, p. 213.
25 Ibid., p. 219.

10

INTIMACY AS DEMOCRACY

A democratisation of the private sphere is today not only on the agenda, but is an implicit quality of all personal life that comes under the aegis of the pure relationship. The fostering of democracy in the public domain was at first largely a male project – in which women eventually managed, mostly by dint of their own struggle, to participate. The democratisation of personal life is a less visible process, in part precisely because it does not occur in the public arena, but its implications are just as profound. It is a process in which women have thus far played the prime role, even if in the end the benefits achieved, as in the public sphere, are open to everyone.

The meaning of democracy

First of all it might be worth considering what democracy means, or can mean, in its orthodox sense. There is much debate about the specifics of democratic representation and so forth, but I shall not concern myself with these issues here. If the various approaches to political democracy be compared, as David Held has shown, most have certain elements in common.[1] They are concerned to secure 'free and equal relations' between individuals in such a way as to promote certain outcomes:

1. The creation of circumstances in which people can develop their potentialities and express their diverse qualities. A key objective here is that each individual should respect others' capabilities as well as their ability to learn and enhance their aptitudes.

2. Protection from the arbitrary use of political authority and coercive power. This presumes that decisions can in some sense be negotiated by those they affect, even if they are taken on behalf of a majority by a minority.

3. The involvement of individuals in determining the conditions of their association. The presumption in this case is that individuals accept the authentic and reasoned character of others' judgements.

4. Expansion of the economic opportunity to develop available resources – including here the assumption that when individuals are relieved of the burdens of physical need they are best able to achieve their aims.

The idea of autonomy links these various aspirations. Autonomy means the capacity of individuals to be self-reflective and self-determining: 'to deliberate, judge, choose and act upon different possible courses of action.'[2] Clearly autonomy in this sense could not be developed while political rights and obligations were closely tied to tradition and fixed prerogatives of property. Once these were dissolved, however, a movement towards autonomy became both possible and seen to be necessary. An overwhelming concern with how individuals might best determine and regulate the conditions of their association is characteristic of virtually all interpretations of modern democracy. The aspirations that compose the tendency towards autonomy can be summarised as a general principle, the 'principle of autonomy':

individuals should be free and equal in the determination of the conditions of their own lives; that is, they should enjoy equal rights (and, accordingly, equal obligations) in the specification of the framework which generates and limits the opportunities available to them, so long as they do not deploy this framework to negate the rights of others.[3]

Democracy hence implies not just the right to free and equal self-development, but also the constitutional limitation of (distributive) power. The 'liberty of the strong' must be restrained, but this is not a denial of all authority – or it only becomes so in the case of anarchism. Authority is justifiable to the degree that it recognises the principle of autonomy; in other words, to the extent to which defensible reasons can be given as to why compliance enhances autonomy, either now or in the future. Constitutional authority can be understood as an implicit contract which has the same form as conditions of association explicitly negotiated between equals.

It is no good proposing a principle of autonomy without saying something about the conditions of its realisation. What are those conditions? One is that there must be equality in influencing outcomes in decision-making – in the political sphere this is usually sought after by the 'one person one vote' rule. The expressed preferences of each individual must have equal ranking, subject in certain instances to qualifications made necessary by the existence of justified authority. There must also be effective participation; the means must be provided for individuals to make their voices heard.

A forum for open debate has to be provided. Democracy means discussion, the chance for the 'force of the better argument' to count as against other means of determining decisions (of which the most important are policy decisions). A democratic order provides institutional arrangements for mediation, negotiation and the reaching of compromises where necessary. The conduct of open discussion is itself a means of democratic education: participation in debate with others can lead to the emergence of a more enlightened citizenry. In some part such a consequence stems from a broadening of the individual's cognitive horizons. But it also derives from an acknowledgement of legitimate diversity – that is, pluralism – and from emotional education. A politically educated contributor to dialogue is able to channel her or his emotions in a positive way: to reason from conviction rather than engage in ill thought through polemics or emotional diatribes.

Public accountability is a further basic characteristic of a democratic polity. In any political system decisions must often be taken on behalf of others. Public debate is normally only possible in relation to certain issues or at particular junctures. Decisions taken, or policies forged, however, must be open to public scrutiny should the need arise. Accountability can never be continuous and therefore stands in tandem with trust. Trust, which comes from accountability and openness, and also protects them, is a thread running through the whole of democratic political order. It is a crucial component of political legitimacy.

Institutionalising the principle of autonomy means specifying rights and obligations, which have to be substantive, not just formal. Rights specify the privileges which come with membership of the polity but they also indicate the duties which individuals have *vis-à-vis* each other and the political order itself. Rights are essentially forms of empowerment; they are enabling devices. Duties specify the price that has to be paid for the rights accorded. In a democratic polity, rights and duties are negotiated and can never be simply assumed – in this respect they differ decisively from, for example, the medieval *droit de seigneur* or other rights established simply by virtue of an individual's social position. Rights and duties thus have to be made a focus of continual reflexive attention.

Democracy, it should be emphasised, does not necessitate sameness, as its critics have often asserted. It is not the enemy of pluralism. Rather, as suggested above, the principle of autonomy encourages difference – although it insists that difference should not be penalised. Democracy is an enemy of privilege, where privilege is defined as the holding of rights or possessions to which access is not fair and equal for all members of the community. A democratic order does not imply a generic process of 'levelling down', but instead provides for the elaboration of individuality.

Ideals are not reality. How far any concrete political order could develop such a framework in full is problematic. In this sense there are utopian elements in these ideas. On the other hand, it could also be argued that the characteristic trend of development of modern societies is towards their realisation. The quality of utopianism, in other words, is balanced by a clear component of realism.[4]

The democratising of personal life

The possibility of intimacy means the promise of democracy: this is the theme I have suggested in earlier chapters. (The reader might like at this point to refer back to the discussion on pp. 94–6.) The structural source of this promise is the emergence of the pure relationship, not only in the area of sexuality but also in those of parent–child relations, and other forms of kinship and friendship. We can envisage the development of an ethical framework for a democratic personal order, which in sexual relationships and other personal domains conforms to a model of confluent love.

As in the public sphere, the distance between ideals and reality is considerable. In the arena of heterosexual relations in particular, as indicated in earlier chapters, there are profound sources of strain. Deep psychological, as well as economic, differences between the sexes stand in the way. Yet utopianism here can again readily be offset by realism.

The changes that have helped transform personal environments of action are already well advanced, and they tend towards the realisation of democratic qualities.

The principle of autonomy provides the guiding thread and the most important substantive component of these processes. In the arena of personal life, autonomy means the successful realisation of the reflexive project of self – the condition of relating to others in an egalitarian way. The reflexive project of self must be developed in such a fashion as to permit autonomy in relation to the past, this in turn facilitating a colonising of the future. Thus conceived, self-autonomy permits that respect for others' capabilities which is intrinsic to a democratic order. The autonomous individual is able to treat others as such and to recognise that the development of their separate potentialities is not a threat. Autonomy also helps to provide the personal boundaries needed for the successful management of relationships. Such boundaries are transgressed whenever one person uses another as a means of playing out old psychological dispositions, or where a reciprocal compulsiveness, as in the case of codependence, is built up.

The second and third conditions of democracy in the public sphere noted above bear very directly upon the democratisation of personal life. Violent and abusive relationships are common in the sexual domain and between adults and children. Most such violence comes from men and is directed towards beings weaker than themselves. As an emancipatory ideal of democracy, the prohibition of violence is of basic importance. Coercive influences in relationships, however, obviously can take forms other than physical violence. Individuals may be prone, for example, to engage in emotional or verbal abuse of one another; marriage, so the saying goes, is a poor substitute for respect. Avoidance of emotional abuse is perhaps the most difficult aspect of the equalising of power in relationship; but the guiding principle is clearly respect for the independent

views and personal traits of the other. 'Without respect', as
one guide to intimacy puts it, 'ears turn deaf, attitudes sour,
and eventually you can't figure out what you're doing living
with someone so incompetent, stupid, unreliable, insensi-
tive, ugly, smelly, untidy . . . It makes you wonder why
you chose your partner in the first place. "I must have been
out of my mind."'[5]

'The involvement of individuals in determining the conditions of their association' – this statement exemplifies the
ideals of the pure relationship. It expresses a prime difference between traditional and present-day marriage and gets
to the heart of the democratising possibilities of the transformation of intimacy. It applies, of course, not just to the
initiation of a relationship, but to the reflexivity inherent in
its continuance – or its dissolution. Not just respect for the
other, but an opening out to that person, are needed for this
criterion to be met. An individual whose real intentions are
hidden from a partner cannot offer the qualities needed for
a cooperative determination of the conditions of the relationship. Any and every therapeutic text on the subject of
relationships will demonstrate why revelation to the other –
as a means of communication rather emotional dumping –
is a binding aspiration of democratically ordered interaction.

Rights and obligations: as I have tried to make clear, in
some part these define what intimacy actually is. Intimacy
should not be understood as an interactional description,
but as a cluster of prerogatives and responsibilities that
define agendas of practical activity. The importance of rights
as means for the achievement of intimacy can easily be seen
from the struggle of women to achieve equal status in
marriage. The right of women to initiate divorce, to take one
instance, which seems only a negative sanction, actually has
a major equilibrating effect. Its balancing consequences do
more than empower escape from an oppressive relationship,
important though this is. They limit the capability of the
husband to impose his dominion and thereby contribute to

the translation of coercive power into egalitarian communication.

No rights without obligations – this elementary precept of political democracy applies also to the realm of the pure relationship. Rights help dissolve arbitrary power only in so far as they carry responsibilities towards the other which draw privileges into an equilibrium with obligations. In relationships as elsewhere, obligations have to be treated as revisable in the light of negotiations carried on within them.

What of accountability and its connection to authority? Both accountability and authority – where it exists – in pure relationships are deeply bound up with trust. Trust without accountability is likely to become one-sided, that is, to slide into dependence; accountability without trust is impossible because it would mean the continual scrutiny of the motives and actions of the other. Trust entails the trustworthiness of the other – according 'credit' that does not require continual auditing, but which can be made open to inspection periodically if necessary. Being regarded as trustworthy by a partner is a recognition of personal integrity, but in an egalitarian setting such integrity means also revealing reasons for actions if called upon to do so – and in fact having good reasons for any actions which affect the life of the other.

Authority in pure relationships between adults exists as 'specialisation' – where one person has specially developed capabilities which the other lacks. Here one cannot speak of authority over the other in the same sense as in parent–child relations, particularly where very young children are involved. Can a relationship between a parent and young child be democratic? It can, and should be, in exactly the same sense as is true of a democratic political order.[6] It is a right of the child, in other words, to be treated as a putative equal of the adult. Actions which cannot be negotiated directly with a child, because he or she is too young to grasp what is entailed, should be capable of counterfactual justification. The presumption is that agreement could be reached, and trust sustained, if the child were sufficiently autonomous to be able to deploy arguments on an equal basis to the adult.

Mechanisms

In the political sphere democracy involves the creation of a constitution and, normally, a forum for the public debate of policy issues. What are the equivalent mechanisms in the context of the pure relationship? So far as heterosexual relationships go, the marriage contract used to be a bill of rights, which essentially formalised the 'separate but unequal' nature of the tie. The translation of marriage into a signifier of commitment, rather than a determinant of it, radically alters this situation. All relationships which approximate to the pure form maintain an implicit 'rolling contract' to which appeal may be made by either partner when situations arise felt to be unfair or oppressive. The rolling contract is a constitutional device which underlies, but is also open to negotiation through, open discussion by partners about the nature of the relationship.

Here is a 'rule book', drawn up in a self-help manual aimed at helping women to develop more satisfying heterosexual relationships. The individual, the author suggests, should first of all catalogue the problems that have arisen for her in previous relationships – those she sees mainly as her own doing and those perpetrated by her previous lovers. She should share the rule book with her partner, who should develop a convergent set of rules:

Rule 1: When I find myself trying to impress a man I like by talking so much about myself that I'm not asking him any questions, I'll stop performing and focus on whether he is right for me.

Rule 2: I'll express my negative feelings as soon as I become aware of them, rather than waiting until they build up – even if it means upsetting my partner.

Rule 3: I'll work on healing my relationship with my ex-husband by looking at how I set myself up to be hurt, and I won't talk about him as if I'm the victim and he's the villain.

Rule 4: When my feelings are hurt, I'll tell my partner how I'm feeling rather than pouting, getting even, pretending I don't care or acting like a little girl.

Rule 5: When I find myself filling in the blanks ['dead' areas in the relationship], I'll stop and ask myself if my partner has given back much to me lately. If he hasn't, I'll ask him for what I need rather than making things better myself.

Rule 6: When I find myself giving unsolicited advice or treating my partner like a little boy, I'll stop, take a deep breath, and let him figure it out on his own, unless he asks for help.[7]

Such a list appears at first blush, not only embarrassingly naive, but also likely to be quite counter-productive. For stating rules as rules, as Wittgenstein impressed upon us, alters their nature. The making explicit of such prescriptions, it can be argued, might rob them of all chance of having a positive effect, since only if they are taken for granted could a relationship proceed harmoniously. Yet such a view, I think, would miss the point. Differential power, which is sedimented in social life, is likely to stay unchanged if individuals refuse reflexively to examine their own conduct and its implicit justifications. Such rules, however unsophisticated they might seem, if successfully applied help prise the individual's actions away from an unconsciously organised power game. In principle, they serve to generate increased autonomy at the same time as they demand respect from the other.

A rolling contract does not deal in ethical absolutes. This one derives from a specific 'relationship problem list' where there were previously 'negatives'. The individual in question felt that she had been overly concerned to impress men in whom she was interested, was afraid to upset her partner by revealing her fears and needs, tended to mother him and so forth. A 'constitution' of this sort, of course, is only democratic if it is integrated with the other elements mentioned above; it has to reflect a meeting of autonomous and equal persons.

The imperative of free and open communication is the *sine qua non* of the pure relationship; the relationship is its own forum. On this point we come round full circle. Self-autonomy, the break with compulsiveness, is the condition of open dialogue with the other. Such dialogue, in turn, is the medium of the expression of individual needs, as well as the means whereby the relationship is reflexively organised.

Democracy is dull, sex is exciting – although perhaps a few might argue the opposite way. How do democratic norms bear upon sexual experience itself? This is the essence of the question of sexual emancipation. Essentially, such norms sever sexuality from distributive power, above all from the power of the phallus. The democratisation implied in the transformation of intimacy includes, but also transcends, 'radical pluralism'. No limits are set upon sexual activity, save for those entailed by the generalising of the principle of autonomy and by the negotiated norms of the pure relationship. Sexual emancipation consists in integrating plastic sexuality with the reflexive project of self. Thus, for example, no prohibition is necessarily placed on episodic sexuality so long as the principle of autonomy, and other associated democratic norms, are sustained on all sides. On the other hand, where such sexuality is used as a mode of exploitative domination, covertly or otherwise, or where it expresses a compulsiveness, it falls short of the emancipatory ideal.

Political democracy implies that individuals have sufficient resources to participate in an autonomous way in the democratic process. The same applies in the domain of the pure relationship, although as in the political order it is important to avoid economic reductionism. Democratic aspirations do not necessarily mean equality of resources, but they clearly tend in that direction. They do involve including resources within the charter of rights reflexively negotiated as a defining part of the relationship. The importance of this precept within heterosexual relationships is very plain, given the imbalance in economic resources available to men and women and in responsibilities for child care and domestic work. The democratic model presumes equality in these areas; the aim, however, would not necessarily be complete parity so much as an equitable arrangement negotiated according to the principle of autonomy. A certain balance of tasks and rewards would be negotiated which each finds acceptable. A division of labour might be established, but not one simply inherited on the basis of pre-established criteria or imposed by unequal economic resources brought to the relationship.

There are structural conditions in the wider society which penetrate to the heart of the pure relationships; conversely, how such relationships are ordered has consequences for the wider social order. Democratisation in the public domain, not only at the level of the nation-state, supplies essential conditions for the democratising of personal relationships. But the reverse applies also. The advancement of self-autonomy in the context of pure relationships is rich with implications for democratic practice in the larger community.

A symmetry exists between the democratising of personal life and democratic possibilities in the global political order at the most extensive level. Consider the distinction between positional bargaining and principled negotiation prominent in the analysis of global strategies and conflicts today. In positional bargaining – which can be equated with a personal relationship in which intimacy is lacking – each side approaches negotiation by taking up an extreme stance. Through mutual threats and attrition, one side or other is worn down and an outcome achieved – if the process of negotiation has not by then broken down completely. Global relations ordered in a more democratic manner would move towards principled negotiation. Here the interaction of the parties begins from an attempt to discover each other's underlying concerns and interests, identifying a range of possible options before narrowing down upon a few of them. The problem to be resolved is separated from antagonism towards the other, so that it is possible to be firm about the substance of the negotiation while being supportive of and respectful towards the other party. In sum, as in the personal sphere, difference can become a means of communication.

Sexuality, emancipation, life politics

No one knows whether at the global level a framework of democratic institutions will develop, or whether alternatively world politics will slide into a destructiveness that might threaten the entire planet. Nobody knows if sexual relationships will become a wasteland of impermanent liaisons, marked by emotional antipathy as much as by love, and scarred by violence. There are good grounds for optimism in each case, but in a culture that has given up providentialism futures have to be worked for against a background of acknowledged risk. The open-ended nature of the global project of modernity has a real correlate in the uncertain outcome of the everyday social experiments that are the subject-matter of this book.

What can be said with some certainty is that democracy is not enough. Emancipatory politics is a politics of the internally referential systems of modernity; it is oriented to control of distributive power and cannot confront power in its generative aspect. It leaves aside most questions posed by the sequestration of experience. Sexuality has the enormous importance it does in modern civilisation because it is a point of contact with all that has been forgone for the technical security that day-to-day life has to offer. Its association with death has become for us as bizarre and almost unthinkable as its involvement with life seems obvious. Sexuality has become imprisoned within a search for self-identity which sexual activity itself can only momentarily fulfil. 'Lay your sleeping head, my love/Human on my faithless arm': so much of sexuality is frustrated love, doomed endlessly to seek out difference in the sameness of anatomy and of physical response.

In the tension between the privatising of passion and the saturation of the public domain by sexuality, as well as in some of the conflicts which today divide men and women, we can see new political agendas. Particularly in its connections with gender, sexuality gave rise to the politics of the personal, a phrase that is misunderstood if tied only to emancipation. What we should rather term life politics[8] is a politics of life-style, operating in the context of institutional reflexivity. It is concerned, not to 'politicise', in a narrow sense of that term, life-style decisions but to remoralise them – more accurately put, to bring to the surface those moral and existential issues pushed away from everyday life by the sequestration of experience. They are issues which fuse abstract philosophy, ethical ideas and very practical concerns.

The province of life politics covers a number of partially distinct sets of issues. One is that of self-identity as such. In so far as it is focused upon the life-span, considered as an internally referential system, the reflexive project of self is oriented only to control. It has no morality other than authenticity, a modern version of the old maxim 'to thine own self be true'. Today, however, given the lapse of tradition, the question 'Who shall I be?' is inextricably bound up with 'How shall I live?' A host of questions present themselves here, but so far as sexuality is concerned that of sexual identity is the most obvious.

The greater the level of equality achieved between the sexes, one might think, the more pre-existing forms of masculinity and femininity are likely to converge upon an androgynous model of some sort. This may or may not be so, given the revival of difference in current sexual politics; but it is in any case devoid of meaning unless we try to specify the content of androgyny, which is a matter of deciding about values. The dilemmas thus raised were hidden as long as sexual identity appeared to be structured in terms of sexual difference. A binary code of male and female, which admits of virtually no mediating instances, attached gender to sex as though they were the same. Gender attributions were then made in the following way:

1. Every individual was assumed to be male or female, with no one 'in between'.
2. The physical characteristics and traits of behaviour of individuals were interpreted as masculine or feminine according to a dominant gender scheme.
3. Gender cues were routinely weighed and assessed, within the confines of permissible gender status behaviour patterns.
4. Gender differences thus constituted and reconstituted were applied back to concretise sexual identities, with 'cross-gender' elements filtered out.
5. Actors monitored their own appearance and behaviour in accordance with 'naturally given' sexual identity.[9]

The force with which these influences are still felt is

indicated by the fact that male transvestism is very commonly stigmatised, even though it is no longer seen in the psychiatric literature as a perversion. More interesting, because it has rather more ambiguity, is the case of women who have or who cultivate the appearance of maleness. Current norms of appearance, demeanour and dress in modern societies permit women a closer similarity to men in these respects than is normally tolerated the other way around. Yet dualism tends to be enforced: if a person is not 'really' a man then she must be a woman. Women who refuse to look 'feminine' find themselves constantly harassed:

> I won't wear dresses and I won't wear makeup, or carry a purse and act more feminine. My boyfriend told me that's the reason I'm being bugged by people, and I know that it is, but I refuse to do that. I wouldn't feel comfortable wearing a dress. I couldn't sit like I'm sitting now. Like you've got to walk a certain way. And makeup's such a bloody nuisance.[10]

A combination of imbalanced gender power and engrained psychological dispositions keeps dualistic sex divisions quite firmly in place; but in principle matters could be organised quite differently. As anatomy stops being destiny, sexual identity more and more becomes a life-style issue. Sex differences will continue for at least the near future to be linked to the mechanics of the reproduction of the species; but there is no longer good reason for them to conform to a clear break in behaviour and attitudes. Sexual identity could become formed through diverse configurations of traits connecting appearance, demeanour and behaviour. The question of androgyny would be settled in terms of what could be justified as desirable conduct – and nothing else.

The issue of sexual identity is a question which demands prolonged debate. It seems very likely, however, that one element might be what John Stoltenberg has called 'refusing to be a man'.[11] Refusing maleness is not the same as embracing femininity. It is again a task of ethical construction, which relates, not only sexual identity, but self-identity more broadly, to the moral concern of care for others. The penis exists; the male sex is only the phallus, the centre of selfhood in masculinity. The idea that there are beliefs and actions that are right for a man and wrong for a woman, or vice versa, is likely to perish with the progressive shrinking of the phallus into the penis.

With the development of modern societies, control of the social and natural worlds, the male domain, became focused through 'reason'. Just as reason, guided by disciplined investigation, was set off from tradition and dogma, so it was also from emotion. As I have said, this presumed not so much a massive psychological process of repression as an institutional division between reason and emotion, a division that closely followed gender lines. The identifying of women with unreason, whether in serious vein (madness), or in seemingly less consequential fashion (women as the creatures of caprice), turned them into the emotional under-labourers of modernity. Along the way emotion, and forms of social relation inspired by it – hate as well as love – became seen as refractory to ethical considerations. Reason cuts away at ethics because of the difficulty of finding empirical arguments to justify moral convictions; it does so also, however, because moral judgements and emotional sentiments come to be regarded as antithetical. Madness and caprice – it needs little effort to see how alien these are to moral imperatives.

Freud rediscovered emotion – through his interpretations of female psychology – but in his thought it remained tied to the dictates of reason, however much cognition was shown to be swayed by the subterranean forces of the unconscious. 'Nothing disturbs feeling . . . so much as thinking': emotion remains the other side of reason, with its causal power increased. No connection is made between emotion and ethics; perhaps they are pushed even further apart, for the theme 'where id was there ego shall be' suggests that the sphere of the rational can be substantially expanded. If ethical imperatives exist, therefore, they are to be found in the public domain; but there it proves difficult to demonstrate their validity and they stand vulnerable to power.

Passionate love was originally one among other passions, the interpretation of which tended to be influenced by religion. Most emotional dispositions can be passions, but in modern society passion is narrowed down to the sexual realm and once there becomes more and more muted in its expression. A passion is today something admitted to only reluctantly or embarrassedly, even in respect of sexual behaviour itself, partly because its place as a 'compelling force' has been usurped by addiction.

There is no room for passion in the routinised settings which provide us with security in modern social life. Yet who can live without passion, if we see it as the motive-power of conviction? Emotion and motivation are inherently connected. Today we think of motivation as 'rational' – the driving pursuit of profit on the part of the entrepreneur, for example – but if emotion is wholly resistant to rational assessment and ethical judgement, motives can never be appraised except as means to ends, or in terms of their consequences. This is what Weber saw in interpreting the motives of the early industrialists as energised by religious conviction. However, in so doing Weber took for granted, and even elevated to the status of an epistemology, what is distinctly problematic about modernity: the impossibility of evaluating emotion.

Seen as a life-political issue, the problem of the emotions is not one of retrieving passion, but of developing ethical guidelines for the appraisal or justification of conviction. The therapist says, 'Get in touch with your feelings.' Yet in this regard therapy connives with modernity. The precept which lies beyond is 'Evaluate your feelings', and such a demand cannot be a matter of psychological rapport alone. Emotions are not judgements, but dispositional behaviour stimulated by emotional responses is; to evaluate feelings is to ask for the criteria in terms of which such judgements are made.

Emotion becomes a life-political issue in numerous ways with the latter-day development of modernity. In the realm of sexuality, emotion as a means of communication, as commitment to and cooperation with others, is especially important. The model of confluent love suggests an ethical framework for the fostering of non-destructive emotion in the conduct of individual and communal life. It provides for the possibility of a revitalising of the erotic – not as a specialist skill of impure women, but as a generic quality of sexuality in social relations formed through mutuality rather than through unequal power. Eroticism is the cultivation of feeling, expressed through bodily sensation, in a communicative context; an art of giving and receiving pleasure. Shorn of differential power, it can revive those aesthetic qualities of which Marcuse speaks.

Defined in such a fashion, the erotic stands opposed to all forms of emotional instrumentality in sexual relations. Eroticism is sexuality reintegrated within a wider range of emotional purposes, paramount among which is communication. From the point of view of utopian realism, eroticism is rescued from that triumph of the will which, from de Sade to Bataille, seems to mark out its distinctiveness. Interpreted not as diagnosis but as critique, as was noted earlier, the Sadean universe is an anti-utopia which discloses the possibility of its opposite.

Sexuality and reproduction in the past structured one another. Until it became thoroughly socialised, reproduction was external to social activity as a biological phenomenon; it organised kinship as well as being organised by it, and it connected the life of the individual to the succession of the generations. When directly bound up with reproduction, sexuality was a medium of transcendence. Sexual activity forged a tie with the finitude of the individual, and at the same time carried the promise of its irrelevance; for seen in relation to a cycle of generations the individual life was part of a more embracing symbolic order. Sexuality for us still carries an echo of the transcendent. Yet given that such is the case, it is bound to be surrounded with an aura of nostalgia and disillusion. A sexually addicted civilisation is one where death has become stripped of meaning; life politics at this point implies a renewal of spirituality. From this point of view, sexuality is not the antithesis of a civilisation dedicated to economic growth and technical control, but the embodiment of its failure.

NOTES

1 I follow closely Held's thought in the first part of this chapter. See David Held: *Models of Democracy*, Cambridge: Polity, 1986.
2 Ibid., p. 270.
3 Ibid., p. 271.
4 Anthony Giddens: *The Consequences of Modernity*, Cambridge: Polity, 1990, pp. 154–8.
5 C. Edward Crowther: *Intimacy. Strategies for Successful Relationships*, New York: Dell, 1988, p. 45.
6 Allison James and Alan Prout: *Constructing and Reconstructing Childhood*, Basingstoke: Falmer, 1990. The 'new paradigm' James and Prout suggest for studying childhood relates closely to the ideas developed here.
7 Barbara De Angelis: *Secrets About Men Every Woman Should Know*, London: Thorsons, 1990, p. 274.
8 Anthony Giddens: *Modernity and Self-Identity*, Cambridge: Polity, 1991, ch. 7.
9 Holly Devor: *Gender Bending. Confronting the Limits of Duality*, Bloomington: Indiana University Press, 1989, pp.147–9.

10 Ibid., p. 128.
11 John Stoltenberg: *Refusing to be a Man*, London: Fontana, 1990.

INDEX

210   INDEX